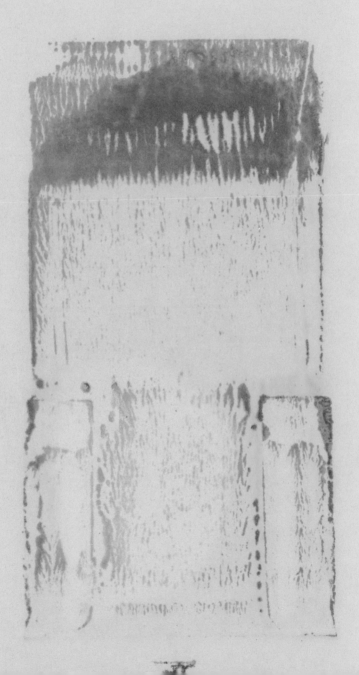

THE MYSTERY AND
LURE OF PERFUME

THE MYSTERY AND LURE OF PERFUME
By C. J. S. THOMPSON

WITH TWENTY-SIX ILLUSTRATIONS

LONDON
JOHN LANE THE BODLEY HEAD LIMITED

Detroit: Reissued by Singing Tree Press, Book Tower, 1969

First Published in 1927

Library of Congress Catalog Card Number 74-75789

FOREWORD

ODOURS and perfumes have had a peculiar attraction for mankind from a period of great antiquity, and their origin in early times was surrounded with great mystery.

The subject is one of profound human interest, especially to students of sociology, and an attempt has been made in the following pages to collect some scattered gleanings of the lore associated with odours and perfumes which have been employed by various races throughout the world. They do not pretend to form either a scientific or technical treatise on the subject.

Acknowledgments and thanks are due to Messrs. J. & E. Atkinson, Bayley & Co., J. Floris, Sainsbury, and Yardley & Co., for their courtesy in supplying information, and to Messrs. Peter Davies, Ltd., and Chapman & Hall for kind permission to reproduce several of the illustrations. We are also indebted to Messrs. Bayley & Co. for permission to reproduce drawings, and to the works of Rimmel, Piesse, and Sawer for some historical details.

CONTENTS

CHAPTER I

THE FIRST GARDEN OF FLOWERS

The Garden of Eden—Where it was situated—The Plain of Eden—The country as it is to-day—A Babylonian description—The first known recipe for a perfume—Myrrh, the earliest known aromatic gum—Kyphi, the famous perfume of ancient Egypt—The presentation of gold, frankincense and myrrh—Onycha—Olibanum from the Land of Punt—Babylonian aromatics . . . . pp. 3–11

CHAPTER II

PERFUMES USED BY EARLY CIVILIZED RACES

Perfumes in ancient Egypt—Recipes recorded in stone at Edfu and Karnak—Customs at Egyptian banquets—The perfume-seller—Cleopatra's love of perfumes—Recipes for making Kyphi—Some celebrated Egyptian perfumed unguents—The beauty of the perfume vessels—How Egyptian women beautified their bodies—Queen Hâtšepᶜu's fleet—Perfumes offered to the gods—Discovered in Tutankhamen's tomb—Use of perfumes at the burial of the dead—Babylonian and Assyrian perfumes—Incense to exorcise demons—Great quantity of frankincense used in ancient Babylon—The temple and the feast of Bel—The Assyrian love of perfumes—King Assurbanipal and his cosmetics—Babylonian market for spices—Assyrian care of the hair—Paints used by women for the face and skin—Antiochus and his love of sweet odours—Perfumes used at the games of Daphne . . . pp. 12–26

CHAPTER III

PERFUMES USED BY THE PERSIANS AND ARABS

The Persians' love for the rose—The perfumes of Araby—
How the Sabians guarded their source—The Arab alchemists—
Distilling perfumes—A wonderful perfumed pie—How the Arabs
preserve their rose blooms—The rose-sellers of old Cairo—
Mohammed and the roses—The Prophet's love for violets—
Flowers prized by the Arabs—Their favourite perfumes—Per-
fumes in shells . . . . pp. 27–37

CHAPTER IV

PERFUMES USED IN EASTERN COUNTRIES

The antiquity of the use of perfumes in India—The oldest
Vedic commentary on sandal-wood—Perfumes offered to the
deities—The roses of Kashmere—The discovery of attar of
Rose—The love of Jasmine—Native sweet-scented flowers—
The fondness of the Muslims for perfumes—Hindu perfumed
unguents—A present for a bride—Favourite perfumes of the
Chinese and Japanese . . . . . . pp. 38–42

CHAPTER V

PERFUMES EMPLOYED BY THE HEBREWS

The perfumes of the Bible—The Holy Perfume—The Holy
Anointing Oil—The Balm of Gilead—Aromatic perfumes used
in purification—Solomon and the perfumes of India—The
ointment of Spikenard—Its identification and origin—Why the
Jews used incense . . . . pp. 43–47

CHAPTER VI

INCENSE AND ITS USE FROM ANCIENT TIMES

The origin of its use—Employed by the ancient Egyptians—
Offerings to Rā—Its use in the temples—How it was prepared
—Incense used by the Babylonians—Fumigation as a method
of expelling evil spirits—Reasons for using incense—Its use
by primitive peoples—Its employment by the Greeks and

Romans—Its use in the Far East—In India, China, and Japan—
Incense used by the ancient Mexicans—Its use in the early
Christian Church—Its use in the Roman Catholic Church—The
Church of England and the use of incense—The composition of
incense—Perfumed candles . . . . . pp. 48-58

CHAPTER VII

PERFUMES USED BY THE ANCIENT GREEKS

Origin ascribed to the gods—General use among the Greeks—
Their love of the odour of violets—Perfumes in Greek
mythology—Plants used by the Greeks for their odours—
Theophrastus on "Odours"—Greek perfumes in the fourth
century—How the Greek perfumers coloured their perfumes—
A famous Syrian perfume—"The Egyptian Perfume"—Scent
phials—Solid perfumes—Apollonius on "Perfumes"—The Rose,
Iris, Crocus, Spikenard, and Marjoram perfumes—The
Athenian perfumes—Extract of Roses of Cyrene—Famous
Greek perfumers—Costly unguent boxes—The perfumers' shops
of Athens—Special perfumes for each part of the body—The
use of perfumes at banquets—Socrates on the love of perfumes
—The use of sweet-smelling flowers and garlands—The perfumed bath—Greek methods of making perfumes—Perfumed
wines—Healing properties of perfumes—Offerings of flowers
to the dead . . . . pp. 59-77

CHAPTER VIII

THE PERFUMES OF ROMAN TIMES

Offerings to the deities—Nero's love of perfumes—Perfumes
in the Roman baths—The use of unguents and scented oils—
The beauty of the baths—How the Romans bathed—Their
favourite odours—Heliogabalus and his love for roses—A "regal
unguent"—The cost of perfumes—Cosmetics and powders used
by Roman women—Juvenal on the use of cosmetics—Poppæa's
bath of asses' milk—Ovid on beautifying the complexion—Face-
powders used by the Roman women—The gift of unguents at
banquets—Odours used in the amphitheatres—Law passed
against the use of perfumes . . . . . pp. 78-87

CHAPTER IX

THE SPICERS OF LONDON

The alchemists and odours—The Guild of Pepperers—The spicers of the Ward of Chepe—St. Anthony, their patron saint—The Spiceries—The Spicers of Bucklersbury—The first record of a perfumer in London—An alchemist on the value of odours—How the alchemists relied on smell—Embalming in England in the sixteenth century . . . . . . pp. 88–94

CHAPTER X

THE PERFUMER'S ART IN ITALY AND IN FRANCE

Venice as the centre of trade—Monks as perfumers—The first perfume laboratories—Santa Maria Novella of Florence—Some famous preparations—Scent boxes—The story of Frangipani—How it originated—Frangipani gloves—The "Golden Rose"—The perfumers of France in the twelfth century—Patents granted by Henry VI—Cosmo Ruggiero—René, the famous perfumer of Paris—The romantic story of Gabrielle d'Estrée—Her death attributed to a perfume—Perfumed fountains—Diana of Poitiers and her cosmetics—Louis XIV and his fondness for perfumes—The "Poudre à la Maréchale"—Ninon de Lenclos and the secret of youth—Madame du Barry and her secret recipes—Cagliostro—Richelieu as a believer in sweet odours—Madame de Pompadour and her bills for perfumes—Marie Antoinette's favourite perfumes—Madame Tallien's bath of crushed strawberries—The first scientific study of perfumes pp. 95–108

CHAPTER XI

THE FRENCH GLOVE PERFUMERS

The antiquity of the craft—How the skins were perfumed—A pair of perfumed gloves for "ye King's most excellent Majesty"—Their introduction into England—Earl of Oxford presents a pair to Queen Elizabeth—The Queen's delight—Her love of perfumes—The Queen's cloak of perfumed leather—Perfumes used in Tudor times—"Casting bottles"—The still-room—Queen Elizabeth's still-room—Rabbard's letter to the Queen—How he extolled his "Waters of odors most sweete"—"A perfume for Queen Elizabeth" . pp. 109-113

CHAPTER XII

PERFUMES OF THE SIXTEENTH AND SEVENTEENTH CENTURIES

Dry perfumes — Damask-water — Lavender-water — "Swete Powder for Bagges"—"A Violette powder used by King Henry of France"—"Chipre"—Perfumes for Queen Isabella of Spain—Powder of Red Chypre—Recipe book of the Duchess of Braganza and the Duchess of Parma—"Damaske perfume" of Master Alexis—"A perfume for the chamber"—"A verie good perfume for gloves"—To perfume garments, sheets, and all other things belonging to a Prince"—"A verie good perfume against the Plague"—To make a perfume necklace—"A sweet-scented bath for a lady" . . . . pp. 114-122

CHAPTER XIII

PERFUMES OF SHAKESPEARE'S TIME

Allusions to perfumes in Shakespeare's plays—His favourite flowers, the rose, lily, and violet—"Casting bottles"—Sweet rushes in church—The smoke of juniper—Perfume bellows—Shadwell's description of a travelling perfumer—"The odour of sanctity" . . . . pp. 123-132

CHAPTER XIV

FUMIGATION BY AROMATIC SUBSTANCES AND THE HYGIENIC VALUE OF THEIR ODOURS

Antiquity of fumigation—Belief in the virtues of strong odours—Fumigation against the plague—Pitch and faggots burnt in the streets—Fumigations during the Great Plague of London—How the Deanery of St. Paul's was fumed—"Angier's Fume"—"Atkinson's Fume"—Tobacco as a disinfectant—"An excellent odour against the Plague"—Aromatics to prevent infection—Flowers in the sick-room—A false rumour—Immunity from disease in flower-growing districts—Chamberland's experiments—Bactericidal properties of essential oils . . . . pp. 133–139

CHAPTER XV

SOME PERFUMED WATERS

English Lavender-water—Perfumes for snuffs and cigars—Lasting odours—Superiority of English lavender—The London lavender-seller's cry—Cultivation of the plant—Distillation of the oil—Hungary Water—Story of its origin—Eau de Cologne—How it originated—The Farinas—Popularity in France—Honey Water—Imperial Water—Florida Water—Perfumes for snuff—How tobacco and cigars are perfumed—Cedar-wood and tobacco—Odour of Russia leather—An ancient perfumed book—The odours of a library . . . . . . pp. 140–150

CHAPTER XVI

PERFUMES OF THE EIGHTEENTH AND NINETEENTH CENTURIES

" A Bill against the lure and fascination of perfumes "—Perfumes of the Georgian era—Beau Brummell on perfumes—Flower cultivation in France—The effect of climate and geographical situation—The perfumer's art—Old London perfumers—Essence of Chypre—Rondeletia—Some old English perfumes—Ess. Bouquet—Ess. Violletta—Wood Violet—White Rose—Moss Rose—Lily of the Valley—Stephanotis—Jockey Club—Millefleurs—Verbena—Heliotrope—New Mown Hay—Ylang-ylang—Opoponax—Jasmine—Jonquil—Peau d'Espagne-Patchouli . . . . pp. 151–161

CHAPTER XVII

PERFUMES FAVOURED BY ROYAL AND DISTINGUISHED PERSONAGES

King Henry VIII's perfume—Queen Elizabeth's perfumes—King Edward VI's perfume—The Emperor Napoleon's favourite perfume—His love for Eau de Cologne—His perfumer's bills—His court perfumers—The Empress Joséphine's fondness for perfumes—King George IV's favourite perfume—How it was introduced to him—An old ledger of a Court perfumer—The King's bill for perfumes—Perfumes for the King and Queen of Hanover—King William IV and his perfume bill—Empress of Russia—Princess Charlotte of Wales—Queen of Wurtemburg—Duchess of Kent—Politicians and the use of perfumes—Queen Victoria's favourite perfume—Queen Alexandra's perfume—Favourite perfumes of Czarina of Russia and Queen Olga of Greece . . . . pp. 162–168

CHAPTER XVIII

ON THE MAKING OF PERFUMES

Methods employed for extracting odours—Separation of odoriferous material—Substances of vegetable origin—Maceration and enfleurage—Plants from which perfumes are derived—The Rose—Legends and traditions—The London rose-seller's cry—The rose fields of Bulgaria—Gathering the roses—Almonds — Balm — Basil — Benzoin — Bergamot—Cascarilla — Cassié — Olibanum — Carnation — Calamus—Geranium—Heliotrope — Ylang-ylang—Jasmine—Lavender—Lilac—Mignonette—Myrrh—Neroli—Orange flower—Opoponax—Orris—Patchouli — Sweet-pea — Rhodium — Storax — Rosemary—Rue—Sandalwood—Tonquin beans—Tuberose—Verbena—Violet—Vitivert—Vanilla . . . . pp. 169–192

CHAPTER XIX

ODOURS DERIVED FROM ANIMAL SECRETIONS

Musk—How it is obtained—Its high value—Adulterations—Hunting the musk-deer—Allusions in early English literature—Countries of origin—Its use in medicine—Ambergris—Mystery of its origin—Its lasting perfume—Civet—Pomet's civet-cat—Dutch merchants and other civet-cats—English civet—Castor—Value of animal odours . . . pp. 193–205

CONTENTS

CHAPTER XX

ARTIFICIAL AND SYNTHETIC PERFUMES

Story of their discovery—Chief classes of synthetic perfumes—Perfumes from coal-tar—How the odour of violets was produced—Chemical perfumes—The derivatives of their odours.
pp. 206–211

CHAPTER XXI

THE PHYSIOLOGY AND PSYCHOLOGY OF ODOURS

The sense of smell—The olfactory nerves—Relation between taste and smell—Sense of smell in man and animals—Sense of smell among primitive races—Repulsive smells—Odours that recall places and events—Subtle odours—Odours that stimulate —Odours that nauseate—Effect of odours on the emotions— Material causes of odours—How odours are conveyed—Sense of smell in animals and birds—The lure and fascination of odours—Odours of animal secretions—Odours of the skin secretions—An uncontrollable lure—Stimulating effect of aromatics—Sir William Temple's experience—Odours that fascinate animals—The wile of the dog-thief—Odours preferred by men and women . . . . . . pp. 212–223

CHAPTER XXII

THE ANTIQUITY OF COSMETICS—ODOURS USED BY
PRIMITIVE RACES

The antiquity of personal adornment—The use of cosmetics by the ancient Egyptians—Assyrian aids to the toilet—Jewish women and their cosmetics—Toilet of the women of ancient Greece and Rome—The use of belladonna—Cosmetics at the Court of Louis XV—The cult of beauty-patches—Preparations of the present day—Face-powders—Lip-sticks—Depilatories— Primitive peoples and their love of strong odours—Oiling the body—Native perfumes—Bridal attire of a lady of Fernando Po—Painting the body—Native customs in the Philippines, Java, and Polynesia—The women of Tahiti—South American Indians and their native perfume—North American Indians and decoration of the face . . . . . pp. 224–238

INDEX . . . . pp. 239–247

xiv

LIST OF ILLUSTRATIONS

THE ORIGIN OF PERFUMES . . *Frontispiece*
(*From an Engraving of the Seventeenth Century.*)

FACING PAGE

A GREEK VASE DECORATED WITH TOILET
SCENES (*about* 400 B.C.) . . . 70

PAGE

ANOINTING THE HEAD OF A GUEST WITH
PERFUMED UNGUENT . . . 13

SLAVES BRING CHAPLETS OF FLOWERS FOR
GUESTS 14

BARTERING A NECKLACE FOR PERFUME . 15

A SELLER OF PERFUMES 18

EGYPTIAN PERFUME BOTTLES . . . 23

HERBS USED BY THE ARABS FOR THEIR PERFUMES 29

AN ARAB DISTILLING PERFUME . . 31

LABORATORY OF AN ARAB PERFUMER . 35

EGYPTIAN KING OFFERING INCENSE TO
HORUS-RĀ 49

PERFUME BOTTLES OF THE HELLENISTIC PERIOD 68

	PAGE
GREEK LADY APPLYING COLOUR TO HER FACE	75
AN EGYPTIAN GARDEN	77
ROMAN PERFUME BOTTLES . . .	83
RENÉ'S SHOP IN PARIS—SIXTEENTH CENTURY	101
A PERFUMER'S SHOP OF THE SEVENTEENTH CENTURY	107
A TRAVELLING PERFUME-SELLER IN THE EIGHTEENTH CENTURY . . .	129
DISTILLING LAVENDER	150
THE LABORATORY OF A LONDON PERFUMER IN THE EIGHTEENTH CENTURY . .	153
THE CARD OF AN OLD LONDON PERFUMER .	161
HUNTING THE MUSK DEER . . .	197
THE MUSK DEER AND CIVET CAT . .	203
SIGNBOARD OF A LONDON PERFUMER IN 1739	223
THE TOILET OF AN EGYPTIAN PRINCESS .	225
ROMAN LADY USING A COSMETIC . .	227

THE MYSTERY AND
LURE OF PERFUME

CHAPTER I

God first planted a garden eastward in Eden.
And out of the ground made the Lord God to grow
every tree that is pleasant to the sight,
And every plant of the field before it grew, and every
herb of the field before it grew.

Genesis, chap. ii.

THE history of perfumes is coeval with the history of man, for from the time of his creation, where'er the sun shone and flowers bloomed, he must have been conscious of sweet odours that gave pleasure to the senses.

The glories of the Garden of Eden have been the theme of poets for centuries, but no more beautiful description exists than that given by Milton in " Paradise Lost ":

> In this pleasant soil
> His far more pleasant garden God ordained.
> Out of the fertile ground he caused to grow
> All trees of noblest kind for sight, smell, taste. . . .

3

Laurel and myrtle, and what higher grew
Of firm and fragrant leaf, on either side
Acanthus, and each odorous bushy shrub,
Fenced up the verdant wall, each beauteous flower,
Iris all hues, roses and jasmine,
Rear'd high their flourished heads between, and wrought
Mosaic; under foot the violet,
Crocus and hyacinth with rich inlay
Broider'd the ground more colour'd than with stone
Of costliest emblem.
                              "Paradise Lost," Bk. 4.

This picture, drawn from the imagination of the blind poet, may be compared with Layard's description of the environs of the ancient city of Nimroud, written some two centuries afterwards, which he believed to be near the site of the Garden of Eden: " Flowers of every hue enamelled the meadows, not thinly scattered over the grass as in northern climes, but in such thick and gathering clusters that the whole plain seemed a patchwork of many colours."

The exact situation of the Garden of Eden has long been a matter of conjecture among archæologists. The Old Testament states it was in the " land of Havilah, where there is gold; and the gold of that land is good: there is bdellium and the onyx stone."

4

The word bdellium has been variously translated as carbuncle and crystal, but the Greek bdellium was the name given to several trees or shrubs
of the genus Balsamodendron, from which an
aromatic gum-resin is obtained, of pungent taste
and agreeable odour.

Sir William Willcocks, who surveyed the entire
region between the Euphrates and the Tigris a few
years ago, came to the conclusion that the Garden
of Eden of the Bible must have been situated on
the left bank of the Euphrates, at the junction of
the two rivers.

" I carefully examined," he says, " the whole
length of the Euphrates from near Anah and Hitt
to the Persian Gulf, to see where gardens could
have been placed, which could have been irrigated
by free flow through the twelve months of the year.
Only two places were found: one was the region
of the cataracts between Anah and Hitt, where I
placed the Garden of Eden of the Semites or
Akkadians, and the other was the marshland begin-
ning near the ruins of Ur of the Chaldees. This
marshland when reclaimed was the Garden of
Eden of the Sumerians.

" I traversed these marshes with translations of
the Babylonian Tablets of the Creation in my hand
and plans and levels before me. Professor Sayce

5

considers that the Babylonian plain was called Eden by its inhabitants, Eden signifying ' a plain ' in the primitive language of the Babylonians.

"It was in this plain the Garden was situated."

In connexion with this, it is an interesting fact, that in the British Museum, there is a Babylonian boundary-stone of a parcel of land situated in Eden upon the Eden Canal.

"To-day, on the Lower Euphrates, you see wide stretches of clover, out of which rise closely-planted date-palms sheltering the ground from the excessive cold of winter and the parching heat of summer. From date-palm to date-palm are festooned luxuriant vines, from which hang rich clusters of purple grapes." *

The Babylonian text states:

"In Eridu, a dark vine grew, planted in a beautiful place,
Embraced by the rivers where the two waters meet."

"Here," says Sir William, "we have the dark vine of Eridu planted in a delightful place and

* "From the Garden of Eden to the Crossing of the Jordan," Sir William Willcocks (1919).

the Paradise of Sumer. The Trees of Life were there sheltering the Garden." *

The use of aromatic gums and sweet-smelling flowers probably dates back to prehistoric man, for from a remote period he must have been aware of the preservative properties of such substances as myrrh, olibanum, and sandal wood.

The first known recipe for a perfume is that given in the book of Exodus, chap xxx. ver. 34, which reads: " And the Lord said unto Moses, Take unto thee sweet spices, stacte and onycha, and galbanum; these sweet spices with pure frankincense: of each shall there be a like weight: and thou shalt make it a perfume, a confection after the art of the apothecary, tempered together, pure and holy: and thou shalt beat some of it very small. . . . And as for the perfume which thou shalt make, ye shall not make to yourselves according to the composition thereof: it shall be unto thee holy for the Lord."

The dried substances were evidently to be first reduced to a fine powder, then mixed together and thus prepared for burning as incense.

Stacte, which means " a dropping," was probably

* This conclusion has since been disputed by other authorities, who state there is no reason for believing that this text contains any allusion to the Garden of Eden.

a variety of myrrh. It is often mentioned by ancient writers, and, according to Pliny, it was a spontaneous liquid exudation of the myrrh tree, more valuable than myrrh itself. Theophrastus mentions a solid and a liquid myrrh, but no drug of modern times has been identified with stacte or liquid myrrh of the ancients; although the statement that 150 lb. of it were presented to St. Silvester at Rome, A.D. 314–335, as an offering from an Egyptian city, shows it was then obtainable in quantity.

Myrrh is probably the earliest aromatic gum of which we have record. It is mentioned in several Egyptian papyri of great antiquity. In a papyrus written about 2,000 B.C., in the Hermitage Museum, there is an account of the writer's journey into Nubia, in which he says: " I will cause to be brought unto thee fine oils and choice perfumes, and the incense of the temples, whereby every god is gladdened. Of myrrh hast thou not much; all that thou hast is but common incense. Ashipu came and delivered me, and he gave me a shipload of myrrh, fine oil, divers perfumes, eyepaint and the tails of giraffes."

In another papyrus found in a pyramid at Cheops, mention is made of myrrh, calamus, juniper, and coriander. It was one of the many

8

ingredients of the celebrated Egyptian perfume Kyphi, used for fumigations, and also in the process of embalming. It is frequently mentioned in the Babylonian and Assyrian cuneiform tablets, and was employed, together with other aromatic substances, for fumigations and incense to exorcise the demons of disease from the body of a sick man.

The fact that, together with gold and frankincense, it formed the offering made to the infant Christ, shows the great value and esteem in which it was held at that time.

In the wardrobe accounts of King Edward I for January 6th, 1299, there is an entry for gold, frankincense, and myrrh offered by the King in his chapel on that day, being the feast of Epiphany—a custom which is still observed by the sovereigns of England.

The identity of onycha has long been a matter of dispute, but it is now generally believed to have been the operculum of a species of sea-snail with a white transparent shell, found on the shores of the Red Sea. It is known as Unguis odoratus, Blatta byzantina, and Nubian women are still said to use it with myrrh, frankincense, cloves, and cinnamon to perfume themselves.

Galbanum, a gum-resin, and the fourth ingredient in the Holy perfume, has been used in

9

making incense from a very early period. It has
been employed in medicine since the time of Hippocrates, and was included in the British Pharmacopœia. It is said to be an ingredient of the incense
still used in the Irvingite churches in London.

The fragrant gum-resin frankincense, or olibanum, is also of great antiquity, and was one of
the most important objects of the traffic which
the Phœnicians and Egyptians carried on with
Arabia. In the temple of Dēr-el-Bahari in Upper
Egypt there are wall-carvings, dating from about
1600 B.C., representing the traffic carried on between Egypt and a distant country called Punt.
A ship is depicted not only laden with bags of
olibanum, but also with olibanum trees planted in
boxes, on a voyage from Arabia to Egypt.

Theophrastus (370–285 B.C.) states that frankincense is produced in the country of the Sabians
occupying the southern shores of Arabia. They
sold it to the Arabs, through whose hands it passed
to the Phœnicians, who acted as distributors to the
temples throughout their possessions, as well as
to the countries with which they traded.

Pliny says that " the Sabians alone knew the
tree which produced frankincense, and of these
only three thousand families, by virtue of heredi-
tary succession. The trees were regarded as sacred,
10

and while pruning them or gathering the gum, men must be kept from pollution."

One of the inscriptions in the temple, referring to the pictures, records that there were " thirty-one verdant incense trees brought among the precious things from the land of Punt for the majesty of this god Ammon, the lord of the terrestrial thrones."

A Greek inscription on the ruins of the temple of Apollo at Miletus records the gifts made to the shrine by Seleucus II, King of Syria (246–227 B.C.), and his brother Antiochus Hierax, which consisted of two vessels of gold and silver, ten talents of frankincense, and one of myrrh.

A far-reaching civilizing influence emanated also from Babylonia to the neighbouring countries where the caravan routes from India, Arabia, and Syria met. The trade in aromatic gums and fragrant oils with Egypt must have begun at a very early period, as a Babylonian clay tablet, still extant, records an order for " oil of cedar, myrrh, and cypress to be obtained from abroad."

These early records prove the great antiquity of aromatic perfumes, and show how extensively they were used in past ages. It is evident that they were regarded of the greatest value and equalled that of the precious metals, gold and silver.

CHAPTER II

THE Egyptians had an extensive knowledge of the properties of aromatic gums and resinous substances over three thousand years ago, and employed them not only for making their perfumes, but also in embalming their dead.

Myrrh, cinnamon, galbanum, and many similar substances are mentioned in the Papyrus Ebers, which was written about 2000 B.C., and a recipe is also given for making pastilles for perfuming the breath.

Recipes for the preparation of perfumes used in the temples are inscribed in stone at Edfu, and a poem has been discovered incised on one of the walls of Karnak, in which Rameses II exhorts the god Ammon to give him victory in battle, with the words: " I have enriched thy domain, and I have sacrificed thirty thousand oxen to thee, with all the sweet-smelling herbs and the finest perfumes."

Perfumes and fragrant gums were held by the

Egyptians in high esteem, and played an important part in their lives.

" The consumption of perfumed unguents and aromatics," says Ebers, " must have been enormous at the highest tide of Egyptian splendour. The people were actually enjoined to perfume them-

ANOINTING THE HEAD OF A GUEST WITH PERFUMED UNGUENT

selves on Fridays. The foods, sweetmeats, and sherbets were flavoured with perfumes, and their fragrance filled the air in every well-to-do house. The women bathed in perfumed water and the men used the scented unguents for their bodies. During great festivals incense was burnt in the streets, so that even the poorest participated and enjoyed the perfumed air.

13

At their banquets the guests waded through roses, and costly perfumes floated in the air. Chaplets and wreaths of flowers were laid upon the altars and offered to the deities, whose statues were frequently crowned with them.

On the occasion of festivals, the guests on their

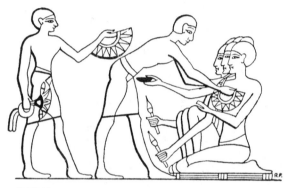

SLAVES BRING CHAPLETS OF FLOWERS FOR GUESTS

arrival were met by slaves, who anointed their heads with perfumed unguents and hung chaplets of lotus about their necks. The apartment was festooned with flowers, and the table and floor were strewn with sweet-smelling flower blossoms.

Maspero, in his account of "Life in Ancient Egypt," describes a market in Thebes, where a cus-

14

tomer is bartering a pair of shoes or a row of enamelled beads, for some perfume from the stall of a seller of perfumes.

"Here," urges the buyer, "is a very strong pair of shoes." But the seller does not require shoes for the moment, so he offers one of his small pots of perfume in exchange for a row of beads.

BARTERING A NECKLACE FOR PERFUME

"It is delicious," he says, "when a few drops are poured out."

The taste for perfumes went on increasing until the time of Cleopatra, whose beauty and charm were said to have been enhanced by the wonderful perfumes which she so lavishly employed on her person. Shakespeare thus writes of her:

15

The barge she sat in, like a burnished throne
Burnt in the water; the poop was beaten gold;
Purple the sails, and so perfumed that
The winds were love-sick. . . .
                                From the barge
A strange invisible perfume hits the sense
Of the adjacent wharfs.

" She used the worth of 400 denarii of spices but
once, to anoint her hands, which was wafted away
on the air and lost for ever."

The most celebrated perfume used by the
Egyptians was Kyphi, for which several recipes
have been discovered. Its fame was so great that
it was adopted and used by the Greeks and the
Romans. It is mentioned by Dioscorides, Plutarch, Damocrates, and Galen. Loret, who made
a special study of it, states that the earliest recipe
consists of the following substances, and it had to
be prepared with great care: Acorus calamus,
Andropogon, Schœnanthus, Pistacia lentiscus,
Laurus cassia, Cinnamomum, Peppermint, Convol-
vulus scoparius, of each equal parts. These were
dried, powdered, and well mixed. The same
quantities of Juniperus phœnicea, Acacia farnesiana, Henna, and Cyperus longus were to be
macerated in wine for a day. Raisins were then
to be steeped in wine for five days and a mixture

16

made of resin terebinth and honey. The ingredients were then to be incorporated and myrrh added, and finally the whole mixed together.

The recipe given by Plutarch contains sixteen ingredients, and includes honey, wine, cyprus, raisins, myrrh, aspalathus, seselis, sthœnanthus, saffron, dock, juniper (greater and lesser), cardamoms, and aromatic reed. He remarks: " Its aromatic substances lull to sleep, allay anxieties, and brighten the dreams. It is made of things that delight most in the night and exhibits its virtues by night."

Damocrates in his recipe includes bdellium, spikenard, crocus, and cassia.

Egypt was also famous for its perfumed unguents, which commanded a very high price. One of the most noted was Psagdi, and the Egyptian oil of lily was also greatly prized and famed even outside the country. Another costly preparation was Qam'ey ointment, two silver bowls of which were presented to a governor of the town of M'e'am by the reigning Pharaoh towards the end of the XXth dynasty. Other favourite perfumes were Mendesium, which was composed of oil of ben, myrrh, and canella; Metopium, which was perfumed with almonds, and contained honey, wine, resin, myrrh, and calamus; Ægyptium,

c

17

which was strongly impregnated with cinnamon and used chiefly for the hands and feet; and Cyprinum, of a green tint, which was extracted from henna flowers.

The most precious unguents often formed part of a large donation and were always included in

A SELLER OF PERFUMES

the complete set of offerings to the shrines of the gods. They were kept in beautiful containers of alabaster or vases of diorite, with stoppers or lids to preserve the contents from deteriorating. According to recent accounts, in some of the magnificent and exquisitely carved alabaster unguent

18

vases discovered in the tomb of Tutankhamen, which is said to date about 1350 B.C., the fragrance of the perfume still lingers after a period of over three thousand years.

Among the many beautiful vases discovered at Luxor was one of great interest, which, on being opened, was found to contain some of the original perfumed unguent that it had held when the tomb was sealed. The vase or jar was of calcite, which had become sealed by natural agency, the changes in temperature and moisture having caused certain salts to crystallize round the lid and so to form a hard protective incrustation.

The contents are described as " rather a sticky substance presenting the appearance of a heterogeneous mixture, consisting of yellow nodules, together with a chocolate-coloured body." It melted partially at the heat of the hand, emitting a faint yet distinctive odour which at first suggested coconut, but afterwards was thought to resemble the flowers of the broom or as being rather valerianaceous in character. Although it had a fatty smell, it was not that associated with advanced rancidity.

The result of an analysis of the substance was given by Chapman and Plenderleith, in a paper communicated to the British Association at the meeting in Oxford in 1926.

They stated that " a careful microscopical examination failed to reveal any traces of vegetable fibre or other organised structures, and that the chemical evidence supported the view that the fat was of animal character. It also seemed to exclude the presence of coconut or palm-kernel oils.

" Having regard to all the results, it appeared probable that the cosmetic consisted of about 90 per cent. of a neutral animal fat with about 10 per cent. of some resin or balsam, and that the smell of the material was probably due to odorous substances formed in process of time from the resins or balsams employed."

It is quite likely that the faint perfume described as being of " a valerianaceous character " is due to Indian nard or spikenard that was frequently employed by the Egyptians in making their unguents, as it is now known to have been obtained from a species of valerian and had a very powerful and persistent odour. There seems little doubt that the preservation of the substance is due to the use of olibanum or other gum-resins having antiseptic properties that were known and used by the Egyptians at that

20

period. In any case, this vase contains the most ancient unguent at present known which has retained its perfume for over three thousand years.

Kyphi was not only used to give an agreeable perfume to the body and clothes, but was also burnt in the house to make it smell sweet, and employed as a medicine.

" The embalming of the dead," says Budge, " was carried out by professional embalmers who were attached to the temples, and all the various objects employed in furnishing the tombs were provided by workmen who were directly under the control of the priests. Their apothecaries supplied the myrrh and cassia to fill the cavity of the body, and the incense, perfumes, drugs, unguents, and oils used in the funerary ceremonies." *

Women of rank and fashion employed fine oils imported from the East, and specially prepared unguents, some of which were scented with strong-smelling perfumes.

Many women thought they beautified their eyes by painting the eyebrows and adding a thick dark line under each eye. Different kinds of eye-paint were used, according to the season of the year, but

* "A Short History of the Egyptian People," E. A. Wallis Budge (London, 1923).

it was thought to be absolutely necessary to anoint the eyelids with one kind of unguent daily.

Some women rouged their cheeks and lips, and the higher classes stained the nails of their fingers and toes a reddish yellow with henna juice. The importance they attached to the artificial beautifying of the body is proved by the fact that after embalmment, the faces of women of high rank were often coloured and their eyelids and eyebrows darkened with antimony.

Hâtšepsu, who reigned as Queen of Egypt about 1600 B.C., despatched an expedition to Punt to bring myrrh and other produce from this remote Sūdānĭ land. Her fleet consisted of five ships, which safely reached their destination; and when the captain, Nehsi, had given to Parahu, the Prince of Punt, the gifts which the Queen had sent, the natives loaded her ships with gold, myrrh, ebony, ivory, boomerangs, precious woods, and incense.

She built the beautiful temple of Dēr-el-Bahari, and decorated the walls with bas-reliefs illustrating her expedition to Punt, which was regarded as one of the most important events of her reign.

Perfumed oils and unguents were offered to the gods in large quantities and a thousand boxes of ointment are mentioned in one instance alone. " Some of the perfume vases were made of

22

turquoise that were used in the mysteries of Osiris at Denderah, and vases of fragrant oils and perfumes were buried with the mummy for his use in the other world. Previous to burial, the body was anointed, perfumed, and crowned with flowers. The ceremony was concluded with

EGYPTIAN PERFUME BOTTLES

1. Dark blue and white glass. 2. Blue, with white and yellow decoration.
3. Green glass decorated in white.

a prayer, in which the 'perfume of Horus' was desired to place itself on the dead man, so that he might receive virtue from the god."

The ancient Babylonians and Assyrians employed fumigations and incense to exorcise the demons of disease in their medical treatment, as

23

far back as 1500 B.C. There are frequent allusions in their cuneiform tablets to the use of the censer, with incantations to drive out the evil spirits. It was also largely used in their religious ceremonies. They erected altars to their gods and offered incense and aromatic substances to them, no doubt carrying on a custom which had come down to them from a remote period. Their knowledge of drugs and fragrant gums was considerable, and in the Assyrian herbal over 200 substances are mentioned.

The Kings of Assyria offered incense and libations of wine to the Tree of Life; and Herodotus states that frankincense to the amount of 1,000 talents weight, was offered every year during the feast of Bel, on the great altar in the temple at Babylon. This magnificent building is described as having eight great towers raised one above the other. The fine statue of the god, which is said to have been of gold, weighed 800 talents, and on the massive golden altar 1,000 talents of incense were burned every year. The Arabs alone furnished an annual tribute of 1,000 talents of frankincense.

The Assyrians were fond of perfumes, and used them to a considerable extent. Luxury appears to have reached its height in the time of Assur-

24

banipal (668–626 B.C.), whose excesses have often been described. He not only painted his face with vermilion and used cosmetics lavishly, but even adopted feminine dress. He is said to have ended his life on a pyre of fragrant woods and was suffocated by their odours.

At an early period, Babylon became the principal market for aromatic gums and spices, and from about 1700 B.C. the Arabs carried on a trade in fragrant gums which continued until the sixteenth century, when the discovery of the Cape altered the traffic of the traders. From Egypt there was a constant demand for these substances, which were used in great quantities for embalming the dead as well as in religious ceremonies.

The Babylonians knew the art of making glass, and kept their perfumes in glass bottles or alabaster vases. They perfumed their bodies and burnt sweet-smelling woods in their living-rooms.

Probably none of the early civilized races bestowed more attention and care to the hair than the Assyrians. The kings usually had a gold thread interwoven with the beard, which, like the hair, was worn elaborately curled. The women wore their hair in long ringlets, confined by a band over the forehead and then allowed to flow over the shoulders. They lined the corners of their eyes

25

and the lids with stibium or kohl, in order to make them appear larger and more brilliant, and they used red and white paint for the face and skin.

According to Athenæus, Alexander the Great had the floors of his apartments sprinkled with perfumes, while myrrh and other aromatic gums were burnt in his halls. Antiochus Epiphanes, King of Syria, carried his love for sweet odours to a still greater extent. In one of the processions during the games held at Daphne, it is recorded that two hundred women were employed to sprinkle the spectators with perfumes from golden vessels. In another procession, boys arrayed in purple tunics, carrying gold dishes of frankincense, myrrh, and saffron, were followed by two incense burners made of ivy wood covered with gold, six cubits in height, and a large square golden altar was placed in the centre. Everyone who entered the gymnasium was anointed with some perfume from fifteen golden dishes, each filled with different aromatics, such as cinnamon, spikenard, foenugreek, amaracas, and lilies. The guests were given a magnificent feast and were crowned with garlands of aromatic plants.

CHAPTER III

THE Persians from an early period have taken especial delight in roses, and at their feasts often spread them as carpets or beds on which to sit or recline. Their love for the rose is shown in the frequent allusions to their favourite flower by their poets and writers.

Sâdî's " Gulistān," the finest poem ever written in the Persian language, is in praise of the rose.

Art thou, then, musk or ambergris, I said;
That by thy scent my soul is ravished?
" Not so," it answered; " worthless earth was I,
But long I kept the roses company;
Thus near its perfect fragrance to me came,
Else I'm but earth, the worthless and the same."

Hafiz also sings of the rose in the lines addressed to his mistress, whom he likens to—

The bloom of the rose when fresh, plucked, and full blown.

27

and again:

Joy round as sweet perfume throws,
Offspring of the blooming rose.

It is probable that the Persians acquired their love for fragrant odours and perfumes from the Medes, who are said to have been inordinately fond of them.

Xenophon records that Cyrus, when twelve years of age, was taken by his mother to see Astyages, King of the Medes. He found him decorated with paint round his eyes, colour on his face, and a magnificent wig of flowing ringlets.

It seems but natural that the Arabs should have had a great liking for perfumes, as their country was the habitat of the majority of the shrubs, trees, and plants that supplied the early civilized world with fragrant aromatic gums and flowers. Thence came olibanum or frankincense, myrrh, jasmine, and the rose. The southern part of Arabia—Sheba or Arabia Felix—was well situated and commanded the main trade-route from east to west of the spice merchants. The great caravan-road was by the valley of the Euphrates to the Mediterranean coast.

The wealth and glory of Arabia Felix, acquired through its trade, was the wonder of ancient times.

28

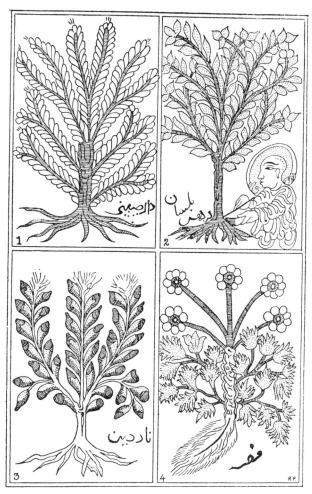

HERBS USED BY THE ARABS FOR THEIR PERFUMES
1. Cinnamon. 2. Balm of Judea. 3. Nard. 4. Indian Nard.
(From an Arab Persian MS., Twelfth century.)

The grandeur of its cities and magnificence of the
abodes of its merchants were renowned. The
Sabians artfully concealed the origin of many of
their precious wares and surrounded their source
in mystery. Thus they gave out that cinnamon was only to be gathered from the nests
of the phœnix, or that it was found in the
land of the birth of Bacchus, in marshes
guarded by winged serpents, also that terrible
bats flew at the eyes of those who tried
to gather cassia, and other fabulous stories, doubtless devised to get a good price for their goods
for which such dangers had to be encountered.

The Arabs learnt the art of chemistry from the
Greeks and did much to develop it between the
ninth and twelfth centuries. They produced several
great physicians, prominent among whom was
Avicenna, called by his countrymen the " Prince
of Physicians," who flourished in the tenth century; also some famous chemists like Rhazes, who
was the first to describe small-pox and measles, and
Jábir-Ibn-Hayyán or Geber, who is said to have
discovered many chemicals in use to-day.

They knew the process of distillation, and it is
to Avicenna we probably owe the first idea of
preserving the volatile oils of flowers by means
of the still. He is said to have been the first to

make Rose-water by this method, which soon became known throughout Europe and the East, where it is still customary to welcome a stranger by sprinkling him with the fragrant liquid. Mohammed encouraged the love of perfumes among

AN ARAB DISTILLING PERFUME
(From an Arab MS., Twelfth Century.)

his followers, which probably accounts to some extent for their extensive use in the countries of the Far East to-day.

In the description of Paradise given in the Koran, it is said that " the ground of this enchant-

31

ing place is composed of pure wheaten flour mixed with musk and saffron; its stones are pearls and hyacinths, and its palaces built of gold and silver." Among the other allurements mentioned are " the black-eyed houris, who will welcome the brave to their bowers, waving perfumed scarves before them." The houris are described as being made of *pure musk*. The fondness of the Arabs for musk is evidenced in the tradition that in the building of two famous mosques, viz. that of Zobaide at Tauris and the mosque at Kara Amed, the mortar is said to have been mixed with a large quantity of musk, so that when the sun shone upon it, the building should become perfumed.

The Arabs also used perfumes in their cookery, as instanced in the wonderful pie that is described by Abd-El-Lateef, of which the following is the recipe:

" Thirty pounds of fine flour are kneaded with $5\frac{1}{2}$ pounds of oil of sesame and divided into two equal portions. Upon one place three lambs stuffed with meat, fried with oil of sesame and ground pistachio nuts, and various hot aromatics, as pepper, ginger, cinnamon, mastic, coriander seed, cumin seed, cardamons, and nutmeg. These are to be sprinkled with Rose-water infused with musk, and upon the lambs are to be placed 20 fowls, 20 chickens, and 50 smaller birds, some of which are to be baked and stuffed with eggs, and some with meat, and some fried in the juice of sour grapes or limes. A number of small meat pies are then to be added and others filled with sugar and sweetmeats. The whole is then to be piled up into a dome, and Rose-water infused with musk and aloes-wood sprinkled over it. Then the other half of the pastry is to be placed over the top and the pie closed and baked, after which it must again be sprinkled with Rose-water infused with musk before it is eaten." Truly a gargantuan pie!

The Arabs have always been passionately fond of flowers, and especially the rose. The Khaleefeh El-Mutawekkel became so obsessed with his love for the flower that he resolved to monopolize roses for himself. " I am the king of the Sultans," he declared, " and the rose the king of sweet-scented flowers, therefore each of us is most worthy of the other for a companion." So roses in his time were nowhere to be found in his territory except in the gardens of his palace. He carried his fondness for the rose to such an extent that he wore rose-coloured clothes and had his rugs sprinkled with Rose-water.

The Arabs preserve their rose blooms by placing a number of buds in an earthen jar and closing the top with clay. The jar is then buried in the earth, and when they want roses, they dig it up and take out some of the buds, sprinkle them with water, and leave them for a short time in the air, until they open their petals in full.

Rose-sellers in the streets of Cairo cry: " The rose was a thorn; from the sweat of the Prophet it blossomed." This old cry refers to the miracle recorded by Mohammed: " When I was taken up to heaven, some of my sweat fell on the earth, and from it sprang the rose, and whoever would smell my scent, let him smell the rose."

Another version of the tradition says: " The white rose was created from my sweat on the night of the Mearaj," the red rose from the sweat of Jebraéel (Gabriel, who accompanied the Prophet), and the yellow rose from the sweat of El-Burák (the beast on which the prophet dreamt he rode from Mecca to Jerusalem previous to his ascension). The favourite flower of Mohammed was henna, which he declared was " the chief of the sweet-scented flowers of this world and the next." Referring to the violet, the Prophet says: " The excellence of the extract of violets, above all other extracts, is as the excellence of me above all the rest of the creation; it is cold in summer and hot in winter. The excellence of the violet is as the

34

excellence of El-Islam above all other religions."

The Arabs make a sherbet from violet flowers and a conserve from the petals with sugar. With them the myrtle is the rival to the violet, for, according to the Prophet, " Adam fell down from

LABORATORY OF AN ARAB PERFUMER
(From an Arab MS., Twelfth century.

Paradise with three things: the myrtle, the chief of sweet-scented flowers in this world; an ear of wheat, which is the chief of all kinds of food in this world; and pressed dates, which are the chief of the fruits of this world."

35

Noamán Ibn-El-Mundhir, King of El-Heereh at the time of Mohammed, monopolized the anemone as a special flower for his own enjoyment. The gilly-flower is highly esteemed for its perfume in Arabia, and three varieties are cultivated—the yellow, which has a delightful scent both day and night, the purple, which gives off its perfume after sunset, and the white.

The narcissus is also much valued. Galen says: " He who has two cakes of bread, let him dispose of one of them for some flowers of the narcissus; for bread is the food of the body and the narcissus is the food of the soul."

Other flowers prized by the Arabs for their perfume are the jasmine, lily, orange-flower, sweet basil, wild thyme, lotus, crocus or saffron, and the flowers of various kinds of bean. They are very fond of musk, and employ civet to perfume the beard or moustache. In their rooms ambergris or aloes-wood is often burned on glowing embers in a censer to perfume the air.

In Eastern Persia and Turkey the living-rooms are still perfumed by the burning of sweet-smelling woods and gums, and it is customary after the bath each Friday to purify the body with scented unguents and cosmetics, the monopoly for making which was at one time held by the dervishes.

36

The Arabs, in ancient times, used to keep their perfumed unguents in beautiful shells chiefly found on the shores of the Red Sea. This practice is alluded to by Horace in the line:

Pour out the perfumed ointment from the capacious shells.

CHAPTER IV

PERFUMES USED IN EASTERN COUNTRIES

THE use of perfumes and aromatic substances by the people of India goes back to the earliest period of their history. Centuries before the Christian era they employed gums and sweet-smelling woods as incense and for perfuming their garments, both in their religious and private ceremonies.

India is rich in trees that yield perfumed woods like sandal-wood and many shrubs and plants from which gums and spices are obtained, such as cassia and cinnamon. Patchouli and the species of valerian from which the highly prized Spikenard is extracted also furnished them with richly scented essential oils.

Sandal-wood is mentioned in the Nirukta, the oldest Vedic commentary known, which was written not later than the fifth century B.C. It is mentioned among the Indian commodities imported into Omana, in the Persian Gulf, in the first century, and the essential oil was used in Ceylon for embalming the bodies of the princes in the

38

ninth century. The Hindus employed it in the construction of their most sacred buildings, and an example still exists in the famous gates of Somnath, which are said to be over a thousand years old.

Gum-benzoin, largely used in India as incense, is obtained from a tree indigenous to Sumatra and Java. It was known to the Arabs as Java Frankincense, and is mentioned in the travels of Ibn Batita, who visited Sumatra in 1325.

An essential part of Hindu worship is the offering of perfumed water for washing the body of the god, as well as sandal-wood, saffron, and " holi " powder.

In the Hindu marriage ceremony, the sacred fire is kept constantly burning by being fed with sandal-wood, perfumed oils, and incense, which give off fragrant fumes. Sweet-smelling woods are also used on the funeral pyres.

Roses are grown and largely cultivated in Kashmere, and the attar from the flowers has been collected by natives for a considerable period.

According to tradition, it was discovered by Noorjeehan Begum (the Light of the World), the favourite wife of Jehan-Geer, who when one day walking in her garden, through which a canal of Rose-water ran, noticed some oily particles floating

39

on the surface. These she removed, and found the odour so delightful that she had means devised to collect it.

The attar, or essential oil, is extracted in the following primitive manner. The flower petals are placed in clay stills with twice their weight of water and then exposed to the air overnight. By the morning, the attar has become congealed on the surface and is carefully skimmed off.

Jasmine, to which the Hindus gave the beautiful name of " Moonlight of the Grove," is a favourite perfume and highly valued. Other native sweet-scented flowers are the pandang, champac, kurna, bookool, and henna, from each of which essences are made at Ghazepore, on the Ganges above Benares.

The Muslims of India share with other Eastern races the love for perfumes. They burn as incense, sandal-wood, aloes-wood, benzoin, and patchouli, and use an unguent perfumed with sandal-wood oil in their religious ceremonies. They employ perfumed powders for rubbing on the face and body, a favourite one being Abeer, which is composed of roses, aloes-wood, sandal-wood, turmeric, camphor, and civet, reduced to powder and mixed together. Another powder used in a similar way is called Chiksa, and is composed of

40

patchouli, sandal-wood, mustard seed, flour, foe-nugreek, cyprus, kus-kus, aniseed, camphor, and benzoin.

A perfumed unguent frequently used, called Urgujja, contains attar of rose, essence of jasmine, sandal- and aloes-woods.

One of the presents a bride usually receives from her bridegroom, takes the form of a toilet-bag which generally contains the following articles: a box to hold betel-nut for chewing, a small bottle of Attar of Rose, a bottle to sprinkle Rose-water, a box for spices, a box for meesu, a powder consisting of galls and vitriol for blackening the teeth (customary for married women), a box for powder to blacken the eyelids, and one for Kajul (similar to Kohl) for darkening the eyelashes, together with a comb and other toilet necessaries.

The Chinese have from ancient times used incense and perfumes in the form of joss-sticks and tinsel-paper, for burning in their temples and on ceremonial occasions. In their houses the incense burner forms part of the domestic equipment.

Musk is probably their favourite perfume, of which they have a direct supply from the musk-deer which are found on their mountains. It is used not only for its odour, but also as a medicine in the treatment of many diseases. Sandal-wood

41

and Patchouli are also among the favourite perfumes used in southern China.

The Japanese employ an aromatic wood called Jinko for burning in their temples and houses, where it is customary to offer incense. They also use a dry perfume known as Nioi-bukooroo. In recent times, however, European perfumes have largely superseded the native products.

CHAPTER V

THE frequent allusions to perfumes and aromatic substances in the Old Testament shows how much they were used and valued by the Hebrews in early times. Besides the Holy Perfume already mentioned, there was the Holy Anointing Oil, the composition of which is given in Exodus xxx. 23-4. It consisted of myrrh, sweet cinnamon, sweet calamus, cassia, and olive oil. This perfumed oil served to anoint the tabernacle, the ark of the Covenant, the altar of burnt offerings, the altar of incense, the candlesticks, and all sacred vessels, as well as being used in the ceremonies of the consecration of the high priests.

The Jewish kings were anointed with it, although it is stated that the kings of the family of David alone had the privilege of being anointed with the Holy Oil.

The custom of anointing a king at his coronation has survived to the present time.

From early times the Jews traded largely in spices and aromatic gums, and Gilead was the home

of many fragrant shrubs and plants. There grew
the tree that yielded the balsam called the Balm
of Gilead, first mentioned in the book of Genesis
in connexion with the Ishmaelite merchants to
whom Joseph was sold by his brethren, who " came
from Gilead with their camels bearing spicery and
balm and myrrh, going to carry it down to Egypt."

Balm of Gilead is a balsam obtained from Balsamodendron gileadense, a tree that grows in
Arabia and near Medina and Mecca. It is said to
be extremely difficult to cultivate, but it was grown
successfully in a garden at Matriya, near Cairo,
from the eleventh to the seventeenth century, when
it was so valued that the garden was completely
walled in and guarded by janissaries. The Balm,
when collected, was stored in the Royal Treasury.
The last tree perished in 1615, through an
inundation of the Nile.

Aromatic perfumes and gums were also largely
used in the purification of women, as laid down by
the Jewish law.

Cleopatra was not the first woman to employ
perfume as an aid to seduction, as it is recorded that Judith, when she went forth to seek
Holofernes, " anointed herself with precious
ointment, and decked herself bravely, to allure the
eyes of all men that should see her."

44

Camphire, which is alluded to in the Bible, has been identified as henna, which is still so largely used by women in Eastern countries for colouring the hair, hands, and nails.

Solomon mentions the Indian perfumes, including cinnamon, spikenard, and aloes, which shows that in his time there must have been trading with the Far East. He also alludes to saffron, calamus, *trees* of frankincense, camphire and myrrh. Spikenard is mentioned several times in the Song of Solomon and twice in the New Testament.

In the first instance, St. Mark records the incident at the house of Simon the leper, " where there came a woman having an alabaster box of ointment of spikenard very precious "; and in the second instance, related by St. John: " Then took Mary a pound of ointment of spikenard, very costly." Both apostles state that the value was three hundred pence, which would be equivalent to about ten pounds of our currency at the present day. The powerful nature of the perfume is evidenced from the statement that " the house was filled with the odour of the ointment." There were several varieties of spikenard, the one with the finest aroma and the most costly being that brought from India, which has been identified by Royle as the product of a Himalayan plant of the valerian

45

order. It is believed to have been an attar which was imported into Rome in alabaster vases, where it was very highly valued and commanded a large price.

Dioscorides and Galen refer to it as Nardostachys, and later it was known as Indian Nard. Pliny gives a recipe for an ointment of Spikenard, which consisted of Indian nard, myrrh, balm, custos, amomum, and other materials; but the " genuine " nard of the Bible was probably the pure attar. He also mentions that Indian Nard in his time in Rome was worth 100 denarii a pound; while Horace refers to " an onyx box of nard that was worth the value of a large vessel of wine."

The Hebrews employed aromatic substances not only for their fragrant odours, but also put them to several other definite uses. They seasoned their meat with spices and flavoured their wines, the women used them as perfumes and fumigated their beds and clothes, and they were employed at the burial of the dead.*

The use of incense by the Hebrews goes back to the earliest period of their history, and was a direct Divine command. " Thou shalt make an altar to burn incense upon. . . . And Aaron

* 2 Chron. xvi.,|14.

46

shall burn thereon sweet incense every morning"
(Exod. xxx. 1–7); "According to the custom of
the priest's office, his lot was to burn incense when
he went into the Temple of the Lord" (Luke i. 9).

Maimonides, the Jewish physician, states that the
use of incense in the worship of the Jews originated
as a corrective to the disagreeable odours arising
from the sacrifice and burning of the animals
offered. The incense was burnt on the "altar of
incense" by the priest every morning. A handful
was also burnt once a year in the "Holy of
Holies" by the high priest, on a pan of burning
coals taken from the altar of burnt offering. It
was also offered in connexion with funeral rites
and in ceremonies held in the house.

CHAPTER VI

THE word perfume is derived from the Latin words *per fumum*, " through smoke," from which it would appear that man's first idea was to offer up the fragrant perfume thus given off, by burning aromatic gums, to his deity. He may have thought that in thus giving pleasure to his god, his prayers would ascend with the sweet aroma from the altar and his supplications be received with greater favour. Thus we find that perfumes in the form of incense formed part of all primitive rites of worship among the earliest civilizations.

The ancient Egyptians offered incense as an important rite, and prayer was made to Rā that he would draw the soul up to heaven on the smoke of the incense. It was the earliest method of perfuming the interior of a building. On the walls of nearly every Egyptian temple representations are to be found of the smoking-censer placed before the presiding deity of the temple. The Egyptian priest is generally represented holding the censer in one hand, and feeding it

48

EGYPTIAN KING OFFERING INCENSE TO HORUS-RĀ

E

with the incense in the form of small pellets with the other.

The Egyptians worshipped Rā at sunrise with an offering of resin, at midday with myrrh, and at sunset with Kyphi, the famous perfume composed of many ingredients already mentioned. The incense burnt in the temples before the altar was made into small pellets or pastilles, and the censer was not swung, but held with the arm outstretched, and replenished with the left hand. It was also burnt in a vessel with a cover perforated with holes through which the smoke could escape, something like the censers in use to-day.

The compounding of the incense was a ritual of importance and surrounded with mystery, the sacred books being read aloud while Kyphi was being prepared in the Egyptian temples.

In Assyria and Babylonia the ancient kings offered incense to the "Sacred Tree," and it was customary to purify the dwellings after sickness with torches and censers. The Babylonians offered incense of cedar, calamus, cypress, myrtle, and fragrant herbs to their deities. Its use is frequently mentioned in their texts, and in one, the King Nabonnedos is described as "filling the temple with the odour of incense."

Fumigation by means of strong-smelling and

pungent smoke appears to have been a method generally employed throughout the world for purifying the person and for driving away all kinds of evil spirits and demons that bring trouble. The Andaman Islanders still believe that the smell of bee's-wax is offensive to the demon that brings epidemic diseases, and that he may be kept away by stakes painted with it. The Kei Islanders of New Guinea also burn the scrapings of buffalo horns to drive off demons, and juniper is burnt by the Indians of Thompson River to keep ghosts from troubling them.

Empedocles of Agrigentum is said to have stopped the ravages of the plague in that city in the fifth century b.c. by having great fires of wood burnt in the streets.

From fumigation with substances that were thought to be noxious to evil spirits to the offering of sweet-smelling odours that would be pleasing to the deities is but a step, and these two fundamental ideas appear to have been common to most races of the world.

Among the reasons advanced as to the origin of the use of incense are the following. First, because the pleasant aromatic odour of which man was conscious was pleasing to the deity. Second, it was used to mask or neutralize the offensive smells of the burning sacrifice and when the dead were buried. Third, it was a medium for prayer, and as the smoke arose, it carried with it the petition to the gods to whom the fragrant odour gave pleasure.

It is worthy of note that the Jews always associated prayer with incense.

Among primitive races the use of incense appears to have been little known. They have, however, the idea that good spirits love the pleasing odour, while evil spirits hate it.

The magicians or witch-doctors of the Malays of Johore burn incense in treating the sick, while it is also offered at their shrines and used in magical ceremonies.

The ancient Greeks burnt sweet-smelling woods like cedar and myrtle in their houses to perfume the rooms, but incense of odoriferous gums was probably not used until the eighth century before the Christian era, when the practice was brought into Greece from Arabia by the Phœnicians. The Greeks offered these fragrant substances to their gods, sometimes without being burned, and presented them in the form of cakes as a separate rite in the cult of various divinities.

They also made sacrificial offerings, not only in the temples but also in their dwellings. Before

52

commencing almost any enterprise, even to start-
ing on a journey, they sought the protection of the
deity most likely to afford safety, and propitiated
by sacrificing an animal consecrated to the particular god. When the victim was laid on the altar,
which was festooned with fragrant herbs and sweet-
smelling flowers, libations of wine were poured out
of a patera and frankincense was kindled; but
occasionally the incense was offered to the deity
alone. Enormous quantities of aromatic substances were thus used at the principal festivals,
and particularly during the Eleusinian mysteries,
which lasted nine days, during which incense was
burnt on the altars night and day.

Among the Romans, twigs of shrubs like myrtle
and cypress were used before aromatic gums came
into use for offerings on the altars; but later, incense was burnt both in public and private ritual
on the altars and in braziers. It is probable that
the use of incense in the Far East is based to some
extent on sanitary principles, as in Europe, at the
time when the dead were buried in the churches, it
was believed that the burning of incense purified
the air and prevented evil emanations.

In India, incense has been employed by the
various races in their religious ceremonies from a
period of remote antiquity. Its use is widespread

53

in connexion with the worship of the gods and the burning of the dead. The fragrant gums from Arabia were brought into the country at an early date, but long before that the Hindus used many of the sweet-smelling woods that abounded in their own land, like sandal and cassia, while benzoin and other gum-resins they obtained in plenty from the Malay and neighbouring countries.

In the cult of Siva, incense is daily offered by the priest before the stone representing the god at Orissa, and perfumes are also placed before it. The Parsees still preserve in Western India the pure tradition of the ritual of incense, as followed by their race from ancient times.

Its use was also continued by the Buddhists, and it is still largely employed in Nepaul, Tibet, Ceylon, Burma, China, and Japan. The Jains, throughout India, burn sticks of incense before their Jina. The substance most commonly used is gum-benzoin, but the consumption of many other odoriferous gum-resins, woods, and leaves is very great. The incense sticks chiefly used are composed of benzoin, aloes-wood, sandal-wood, rock lichen, patchouli, rose, and gum-mastic.

The Muslims of India burn incense at the ceremonies of circumcision, virginity, and marriage, and also at their funerals.

54

In Tibet it is used at the initiation ceremony of a monk, and is daily offered to the good spirits and to Lamas in the monasteries. It is prominent in the festivals and exorcisms, and is also burned before the Lamas at the performance of religious dramas.

Perfumes and incense form one of the five sensuous offerings, and also the " presentation of offerings," which is one of the seven steps of worship. Because of the belief that it will ward off evil spirits, the Tibetans often place some incense in the amulet boxes they commonly wear, and in which they have great faith for preserving them from bodily harm.

In China, incense is universally used both in the temples and in the houses, as part of the daily worship. It is also employed when consulting the gods and in magical rites. The great sacrifice of the Kau dynasty began with libation of fragrant millet spirit to attract the divinities or spirits worshipped, and to secure their presence at the rite.

In Japanese Buddhism, incense is commonly used and has influenced the native Shinto religion, where it is now burnt in censers at many of their ceremonies.

The use of incense was not confined to the races of the Old World, as the ancient Mexicans offered it to all their gods and used it in processions, at festivals, and at their sacrifices. It was offered four times daily in their temples, and Quetzalcoatl, one of their greatest deities, is said to have delighted in fragrant perfumes and odours. The incense was carried in an embroidered bag and thrown on an open censer of baked clay containing fire. Copal gum was employed, together with a native herb called yiauhtli, which was believed to have a narcotic effect upon those who inhaled it. The apartments in the royal palace were perfumed with the odour from numerous censers in which spices and perfumes were burned; and at banquets, among the Nahuas, the guests were given reeds filled with aromatic herbs which were burned to diffuse fragrance, the smoke being inhaled. Tobacco mixed with oil of amber and sweet-smelling leaves were also used in a similar way.

Incense does not appear to have been used in the Christian Church before the fourth century, when it is said to have been burnt in the first Christian services held in the catacombs of Rome, and then probably for sanitary reasons. The Pseudo-Dionysius, referring to the vigil offices on Sunday in Jerusalem, alludes to the priest censing the altar and making the circuit of the holy place. In the benediction of the incense used in the time of Char-

56

lemagne occur the words, " May the Lord bless this incense to the extinction of every noxious smell, and kindle it to the odour of its sweetness," which leaves no doubt as to its use at that period. In the eighth century it is mentioned in connexion with the procession of the Pontiff and his acolytes from the sacristy to the altar in the church at Rome. Its further use was evidently gradual and its general employment in the service of the Church was probably not before the fourteenth century.

Perfumes were not only used in the early Church in the form of incense, but were also sometimes mixed with the oil and wax employed for the lamps and candles.

Constantine the Great provided fragrant oils for burning on the altars of some of the churches in Rome, and St. Paulinus of Nola, writing in the fifth century, states that wax tapers were made for use in the churches.

In the Church of England its use was gradually abandoned after the reign of Edward VI, but it has never been abolished by law. In the Roman Catholic Church it is burned at Solemn Mass, at the Gospel, Offertory, and Elevation, at solemn blessings, processions, choral offices, consecration of churches, and other rites.

There is still some mystery made as to the composition of incense used at the present time. It varies considerably in composition, but the chief aromatic ingredients are usually gum-benzoin and sandal-wood. The following formula is one that is frequently employed. Take of—

Gum-benzoin in powder . .	4 oz.
Cascarilla bark . . .	4 oz.
Sandal-wood	8 oz.
Vitivert	1 oz.
Potassium nitrate . . .	1 oz.
Musk	8 gr.
Balsam of tolu	1 oz.

Mix the powders thoroughly and sieve before using.

The burning of fumigating pastilles and " aromatic ribbon " in sick rooms to-day is but a survival of the practice of masking offensive odours by the use of stronger ones, as employed centuries ago.

CHAPTER VII

A T an early period of their culture the Greeks developed a great liking for perfumes, and the art of the perfumer became one of importance in ancient Greece. They ascribed perfumes to a divine origin, and their poets make constant allusions to the gods who delighted in delicious odours which were dedicated to their use. Thus Homer refers to Juno:

Here first she bathes, and round her body pours
Soft oils of fragrance and ambrosial showers.

In Greek mythology the origin and use of perfumes is attributed to the Immortals, and, according to the legends, man derived his knowledge of them from the indiscretion of Æone, one of the nymphs of Venus.

Like other races of antiquity, the Greeks appear to have practised the anointing of the bodies of their dead. Thus Homer sings:

59

Venus night and day,
Daughter of Jove,
All the corpse o'erlaid with roseate oil
    Ambrosial.

In another allusion to perfumes, he says:

Spirit divine, whose exhalation greets
The sense of gods with more than mortal sweets.

Criton, before Galen's time, introduced perfumes for medicinal purposes and fumigations became popular. Hippocrates is said to have freed
Athens from the plague by using fumigations of
aromatic plants. It has been stated that during
epidemics of cholera in Paris and London, working perfumers have remained immune to the
disease.

By the time Greek civilization reached its zenith,
the art of blending, making, and using perfumes
had rapidly developed and had become a feature
of everyday life. Nearly every Greek author or
historian makes some reference to the use and
abuse of perfumes, which had indeed been brought
to a fine art.

They offered perfumes and essences to their
deities and to their honoured dead; they crowned
themselves with roses at their banquets, placed

60

perfume-boxes in their dining-halls, and impregnated their food and wines with fragrant odours. For the latter purpose they chiefly employed roses and violets. They kept their robes in chests of perfumed woods, and the leaders of fashion used a special scent for each part of the body. Thus unguents for the head were perfumed with marjoram, palm oil was used for the face and chest, essence of ground-ivy for the neck and lower limbs, while mint was preferred for the arms.

The odour of violets was a favourite with the Greeks, and various blends of mints and thyme were also very popular.

The lure of perfumes eventually carried them to such an extent that Solon promulgated a law interdicting the sale of fragrant oils to the men of Athens.

Theophrastus, the Greek " Father of Botany," who was born at Eresos in Lesbos in the year 370 B.C., has left on record a very interesting account of the various plants used for their perfumes in his time. He mentions Cassia, Cinnamon, Cardamoms, Spikenard, Balsam of Mecca, Aspalathos, Storax, Irisnarte, Kostos, All-heal, Saffron, Crocus, Myrrh, Kypeiron, Ginger-grass, Sweet Flag, Sweet Marjoram, Lotus, and Dill.

He states that " some of them grow in many

places, but the most excellent and most fragrant of all come from Asia and sunny regions. From Europe come none of them except the iris."

In one of his minor works, entitled "Concerning Odours," he gives a remarkable descriptive account of the perfumes used at that early period and shows a considerable knowledge of physiology. "Earth," he states, "is the only elementary substance which has a smell, or at least has one to a greater extent than others, because it is of a more composite character. Anything which is decomposing has an evil odour." He recognized that every "plant, animal, or inanimate thing has an odour and one peculiar to itself, but in many cases it is not obvious to us. Thus things which appear to us to have no odour give forth one of which other animals are conscious. Things which have a good odour are often unpleasant, astringent, or somewhat bitter to the taste. The two senses of taste and smell being akin to each other, wherefore it is through things which appeal to the taste as well as those which appeal to the sense of smell that men try to discover fragrant odours."

He raises an interesting question in asking why it is that, while "the smell of flowers and other things used for making garlands can be perceived at a greater distance, the iris perfume, spikenard and other fragrant odours smell stronger at a short distance?" He advances the theory that "the perfume of flowers is on the surface, while that of roots and gums is in the solid and dried up, so the latter require a gentle heat, which by gradually warming them will cause the scent to be exhaled."

He says the perfumer's aim in the preparation of perfumes should be to make the odours lasting, and that is why men make oil the vehicle of them. He recommends olive oil pressed from coarse olives for this purpose, but "best of all is the oil from the Egyptian or Syrian balanos, which keeps the longest; while sesame oil receives rose perfume better than any other."

We owe to Theophrastus the names of the various perfumes used by the Greeks in the fourth century B.C. The first mentioned is Kypros, which was perfumed with cardamoms; Aspalathos was another, and Rose, in which a large quantity of salt was used, probably to bring out the perfume of the petals. Rose and Gillyflower perfumes were made from the flowers, and a perfume called Susinon was prepared from lilies. Quince perfume was made by macerating the fruit in oil, Myrtle and Dropwort from the leaves of the plants, and Iris, Spikenard, and Sweet Marjoram from their roots.

63

A celebrated Greek perfume was called Megaleion, which was sold at a very high price. It was composed of cassia, cinnamon, myrrh, burnt resin, and oil of balanos.

The Greek perfumers sometimes coloured their perfumes, thus Sweet Marjoram, Rose, and Megaleion were tinted pink by means of alkanet root and a substance called khroma, a root imported from Syria.

Several perfumes were valued for their medicinal properties, among them being Megaleion, which was said to " relieve the inflammation caused by any wound." It was very difficult to compound and costly to make, the oil of balanos having to be boiled for ten days and nights before the resin and other ingredients were added. The myrrh had to be bruised and the oily part called stakte collected, which was then mixed with the cinnamon and cassia and incorporated with the other substances.

The " Egyptian perfume," which was also very valuable, contained myrrh and cinnamon, and was said to last longer than any other, with the exception of Iris.

According to Theophrastus, " A certain perfumer said that he had had Egyptian perfume in his shop for eight years and Iris perfume for twenty,

64

and that they were still good, and in fact better than when fresh." The perfumes made direct from the flowers were Rose, Gillyflower, Lilies (called Susinon), Bergamot, Mint, Tufted Thyme, Kypros, and Saffron or Crocus.

The Greeks believed that excessive cold and heat caused perfumes to deteriorate, and " that is why men put them into vessels of lead and phials of alabaster."

The Academy of Inscriptions of Paris possess a small phial of alabaster, bearing the words, " Cinnamon from Krinippos," the latter being the name of a renowned perfumer of ancient Greece. " Headache," says Theophrastus, " is caused by Sweet Marjoram, Spikenard, and Megaleion among costly perfumes, and most of the cheap ones have also this effect," which might truly be said of their counterparts to-day. " The lightest are Rose, Kypros, and Lily, which seem best suited for men; while Myrrh Oil, Megaleion, the " Egyptian perfume," Sweet Marjoram, and Spikenard are lasting, and what women require. The spices of the solid perfumes if moistened with fragrant wine last a long time. They are used to impart a pleasant odour to clothes, while the powders are used for bedding, so that they may come in contact with the skin, for this kind of preparation gets a better hold and is more lasting, men use it thus, instead of scenting their bodies directly. It is to be expected that perfumes should have medicinal properties in view of the virtues of their spices. The effect of plasters and of what some call poultices prove these virtues, since they disperse tumours and abscesses and produce a distinct effect on the body and also its interior parts. If one lays a plaster on his abdomen and breast, he produces fragrant odours in his breath."

We owe another account of the sources of some of the perfumes used by the Greeks to Apollonius of Herophila, who wrote a treatise on perfumes. " Iris," he states, " is best in Elis and Cyzicus; the perfume made of roses is most excellent at Phaselis, and that made at Naples and Capua is also very fine. That made from crocus or saffron is in the highest perfection at Soli in Cilicia and Rhodes. The Essence of Spikenard is best at Tarsus and the Extract of Vine Leaves at Cyprus and Adramyttium. The best perfume from marjoram comes from Kos, but Egypt bears the palm for the Essence of Cypirus, and the next best is the Cyprian and Phœnician, and after them the Sidonian.

" The perfume called Panathenaicum is made at Athens, and those called Metopian and Men-

66

desian are prepared with the greatest skill in Egypt, where the Metopian is made from an oil which is extracted from bitter almonds. Still, the superior excellence of each perfume is owing to the purveyors and the materials and the artist and not to the place itself, for Ephesus formerly, as men say, had a high reputation for the excellence of its perfumery and especially of Megaleion, but now it has none. The finest Extract of Roses in the world was made at Cyrene, while the great Berenice was alive. Long ago there used to be a most delicious unguent extracted from frankincense at Pergamus, owing to the invention of a certain perfumer of that city, for no one else had ever made it before him, but now none is made there."

Some of the more famous Greek perfumers' names are perpetuated in the names of their perfumes.

Thus Megallus, the originator of Megaleion, is alluded to:

And say you are bringing her such unguents
As old Megallus never did compound.

Peron was another celebrated Athenian perfumer who is mentioned in the following lines.

I left the man in Peron's shop just now
Dealing for ointment; when he has agreed
He'll bring your Cinnamon and Spikenard Essence.''

The boxes or containers of alabaster for the

PERFUME BOTTLES OF THE HELLENISTIC PERIOD

unguents were often very beautifully decorated,
and some of the specimens that have come down
to us are gems of Greek art. Many were of considerable value and carved in onyx and other costly
stones.

68

The shops of the perfumers in Athens became the meeting-place for all classes of society. They were frequented by statesmen, philosophers, artists, and men of fashion, who met and discussed affairs of State, gossip, scandal, and the latest fashionable intelligence.

Special perfumes were often used for certain parts of the body on account of their remedial virtues. Thus the Essence of Quince was said to be good for the dyspeptic, the Vine-leaf perfume was used to clear the mind, and the perfume of White Violets was considered good for the stomach. Ginger-grass was said to have a more biting quality than Sweet Flag, but both were regarded as being equally astringent.

" Perfumes," says Apollonius, " appear sweetest when the scent comes from the wrist, so that perfumers apply scent to this part. Heat changes or destroys the character of a scent, and the effect on the sense of smell is immediately perceived when perfumes are brought into close contact with the skin."

Athenæus, who flourished about A.D. 228, records that the Carmini at their banquets, after pledging one another in wine, anointed their heads with unguents, especially that made from roses, and " if they cannot get that, with one made from

69

apples, in order to ward off the effects of the liquor. If they cannot get apples, they then use that extracted from the iris or from spikenard."

Thus Alexis aptly says:

His nose he anoints, and thinks it plain
'Tis good for health with scents to feed the brain.

This custom of anointing the head at banquets is said to have arisen from an idea that the heating effects of wine could be better borne if the head was wet.

Socrates strongly disapproved of the inordinate love of perfumes manifested by his fellow-countrymen. " No man," he says, " is ever anointed with perfume for the sake of men, and as to women, how can they want perfume in their husbands when they themselves are redolent of it ? " If a slave and a freeman be anointed with perfume, they both smell alike in a moment, but those smells which are derived from free-labours require both virtuous habits and a good deal of time, if they are to be agreeable and in character with a freeman."

The Greeks were extremely fond of sweet-smelling flowers. Lovers festooned the doors of their mistresses' houses and crowned the heads of

70

A GREEK VASE DECORATED WITH TOILET SCENES

their guests at table with garlands. Of this custom
Sappho sings:

But place those garlands on the lovely hair,
Twining the tender sprouts of anise green
With skilful hand; for offerings of flowers
Are pleasing to the gods, who hate all those
Who come before them with uncrowned heads.

Philonides the physician, in his treatise on
unguents and garlands, states that a certain man
having a headache pressed his head and found relief, and so invented a ligature as a remedy for
headache. " Thus they took to binding the head
with garlands and crowns of myrtle, to repress the
rising fumes of wine, and garlands of roses to
relieve headache and give coolness." In this we
probably have the origin of the use of a wet towel
by the student who burns the midnight oil.

The most suitable flowers for use as garlands are
mentioned in the Cyprian poems, as follows:

In crocus, hyacinth and blooming violet,
And the sweet petals of the peerless rose,
So fragrant, so divine, nor did they scorn
The dewy cups of the ambrosial flower
That boasts Narcissus' name—such robes, perfumed
With the rich treasures of revolving seasons,
The golden Venus wears.

Athenæus mentions that in Alexandria a garland was used made of the lotus flower called the Garland of Antinous. The entrance of garlands and perfumes borne by the slaves in vessels of gold and alabaster vases into the banqueting-room heralded the approach of the second course. Nicostratus says:

Be sure and have the second course quite neat;
Adorn it with all kinds of rich confections,
Perfumes and garlands, aye and frankincense,
And girls to play the flute.

Two other perfumes favourite with the Greeks were Baccaris and Psagdi, the former being an unguent from the crocus and the latter being made in Egypt.

The perfumed bath affected at this period is thus described by Antiphanes:

In a large gilded tub he steeps his feet
And legs in rich Egyptian unguents,
His jaws and breasts he rubs with thick palm oil,
And both his arms with extract sweet of mint,
His eyebrows and his hair with marjoram,
His knees and neck with essence of ground-thyme.

Such was the bath of the Athenian man of fashion.

72

Xenophanes thus records the customary procedure at a Greek banquet:

A willing youth presents to each in turn
A sweet and costly perfume; while the bowl,
Emblem of joy and social mirth, stands by,
Filled to the brim; another pours out wine
Of most delicious flavour, breathing round
Fragrance of flowers, and honey newly made,
So grateful to the sense, that none refuse,
While odoriferous gums fill all the room.

An ingenious method of diffusing perfume throughout the banqueting-hall is thus described:

He slipped four doves, whose wings were saturate
With scents, all different in kind—these doves,
Wheeling in circles round, let fall upon us
A shower of sweet perfumery, drenching, bathing,
Both clothes and furniture and lordlings all.
I deprecate your envy when I add,
That on myself fell floods of violet odours.

As alcohol, the usual solvent employed at the present time for essential oils in making perfumes, was unknown to the Greeks, fixed oils and wine were employed as vehicles for the purpose. In making their dry perfumes, they simply reduced

73

the roots and other substances to powder and mixed them together. " As to the mixing of solid substances," says a Greek writer, " in making powders and compound perfumes, the more numerous and more various the perfumes that are mixed, the more distinguished and the more grateful will be the scent. The custom is to use a mixture made of all kinds, the aim and object being to produce a general scent derived from them all.

" Compound perfumes are made from aromatic gums; they bruise and mix a variety of these and shut them up in a box and take out the one that seems to have the strongest smell. This treatment is repeated at intervals, so that the smell of no one ingredient may overpower the others, and clothes put away with such perfumes acquire a marvellous fragrance.

" The Egyptian perfume, Myrrh Oil and others that have a strong odour, become sweeter if they are mixed with fragrant wine, and myrrh itself is made to exhale a more fragrant odour by being steeped in sweet wine."

The Greeks used certain aromatic perfumes to impart a bouquet or sweet flavour to their wines. " Thus," says Theophrastus, " the wine that is served in the Town Hall of Thasos, which appears to be of wonderfully delightful quality, is thus

74

flavoured. They put into the jar a lump of dough which has been kneaded up with honey, so that the wine gets its fragrance from itself, but its sweet taste from the honeyed dough."

The medicinal properties attributed to some per-

GREEK LADY APPLYING COLOUR TO HER FACE

fumes no doubt added to their popularity. Recipes for healing essences and cosmetics are recorded on the ex-votive tablets in the temples of Asklepios, where the attendants employed them in their treat-

75

ment of the sick. Anacreon thus alludes to the rose:

The rose distils a healing balm
The beating pulse of pain to calm.

The soothing properties of rose-water are appreciated to-day, as it is still used frequently as a vehicle for applications to the skin and to the eyes.

The ancient Greeks carried on the Egyptian custom of placing flowers on the graves and tombs of the dead. Perfumes also played an important part in funeral ceremonies, and incense was thrown when the bodies of the dead were consumed by fire.

The custom of offering flowers to the dead, which still survives, appears to have been world-wide from a time of great antiquity, and is thought to have arisen in the belief that since flowers and their odours were pleasing to man, their fragrance would be acceptable to the deities.

The ancient Egyptians and the Babylonians placed flowers on their dead, and in Buddhism the practice is general and dates from an early period.

In Japan, in the domestic rites of Shinto, vases of flowers stand on the " god-shelf " or shrine. The Aztecs placed flowers on the graves of their dead for a period of four years, during which time

76

the souls were believed to be passing their preparatory stages in heaven. The Muslims put sweet basil and other flowers on their tombs during the two great festivals of the year, while the early Christians retained the custom of strewing flowers on their graves.

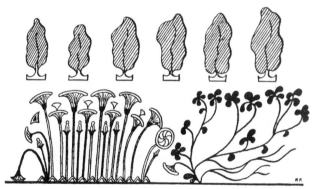

AN EGYPTIAN GARDEN
(From a Wall Painting at Thebes.)

CHAPTER VIII

THE PERFUMES OF ROMAN TIMES

IN the early days of ancient Rome and before the luxurious habits and customs of the Greeks had been adopted, the people employed the wild flowers and herbs as offerings to their deities. Ovid states,—

The simple savin on the altars smoked,
A laurel sprig the easy gods invoked,
And rich was he whose votive wreath possessed
The lovely violet with sweet flowers dress'd.

It was not until about the fifth century that the use of perfumes became popular in Rome, and the craze reached its height during the period of the Empire.

Caligula, Nero, and other emperors spent enormous sums of money on fragrant gums and perfumes. At the funeral of Poppæa, Nero is said to have used more perfumes and incense than could be produced in one year in Arabia, the country, at that time, from which they obtained their supplies.

The perfumers or myrepsi formed a flourishing industry. The Roman patrician anointed himself three times a day with rare perfumed oils and unguents, which his slaves would transport with him to the baths in costly vessels of beautiful workmanship.

The baths of ancient Rome formed part of the extensive buildings called the Thermæ, which were an important feature of every great city and formed a general meeting-place or rendezvous of social life.

The Thermæ of Caracalla and many of the others were divided into three main parts. The great central structure contained the Tepidarium or warm-lounge, the Calidarium or hot-room, with a hot-water bath, the Sudatorium or hottest room, and the Frigidarium or cold room, with its piscina or swimming-bath attached. Adjoining these were dressing-rooms, and the Unctuarium for anointing the body of the bather with perfumed unguents, which were kept in beautiful vases of alabaster on the shelves. Here also the aliptor performed his duties of massaging, sanding, or scraping the skin with the strigil. A Spæristerium for games of ball, a library, and a small theatre were sometimes included in the central building. A park-like enclosure surrounded the structure,

79

which was planted with trees and ornamented with statuary and fountains, part of which was used as a Stadium for the athletic games and sports.

The internal decorations were on the most lavish scale. The walls were usually of costly marbles or decorated with exquisite mosaics. The roof with arched domes was supported on graceful pillars, while the baths were built of white marble, into which the water flowed through beautifully wrought taps of silver or bronze. The corridors were lined with fine statuary and supported by ornamental columns of graceful design.

The outer ring of the buildings included lecture-rooms and apartments for the philosophers, poets, and statesmen who frequented the Thermæ, while round it were colonnades which served as a protection from the sun. In the front were shops and accommodation for the numerous slaves of the establishment.

Let us follow the bather as he passes through the central porch and across the promenade, 130 feet wide, planted with trees, and enters the main building or baths proper, through one of the four doorways to the dressing-room, where he hands his robes over to the attendant slaves. He then descends into the cold swimming-bath by two marble steps. The bath is fed by perpetual streams of running water, that issue from the mouths of lions sculptured in marble or wrought in brightly polished silver, which, as it splashes into the bath, produces a delicious air of coolness in hot and sultry weather. He next proceeds to the Tepidarium, heated with hot air from furnaces below, and furnished with charcoal braziers and benches to rest upon. Here the walls are beautifully decorated with mosaics, paintings of symbolic scenes, or elaborate designs in glowing colour. Then if he wishes, he enters the Calidarium or sweating room, constructed with double walls and floor, between which hot air is passed. When leaving, cold water is splashed over his head from the labrum, by a slave. Finally, he resigns himself to the care of the attendants in the Unctuarium, where he is massaged, scraped, and the whole of his body anointed or rubbed with perfumed oils.

The perfumes chiefly used by the Romans were the solid unguents, made with a basis of some fat which acted as a solvent for the substance used to scent them; and the liquid, in which oils like balanum were employed as the vehicle. The dry or powdered materials were also used in the houses for perfuming the rooms or placing among clothes, beds, and wall-hangings.

The solid unguents were usually perfumed with

G

a single odour, such as rose, narcissus, quince, or other flowers, but sometimes blended perfumes were employed. Of these, Susinon, which was made with lilies, oil of ben, calamus, honey, cinnamon, saffron, and myrrh, was a favourite, also Nardinum, consisting of sweet rush, oil of ben, cistus, spikenard, amomum, myrrh, and balm.

Pliny records a recipe for a " regal unguent " containing twenty-seven ingredients, which, he says, was originally prepared for the King of the Parthians.

Some of these preparations were very expensive and cost about £14 a pound. They were applied to the whole body, as well as the hair and the soles of the feet.

The containers for liquid perfumes were of glass or alabaster, while the solid unguents were kept in fairly large vases or pots of terra cotta or alabaster, the lids being sometimes beautifully decorated with figures and designs modelled in relief. Like the Greeks, the Romans used perfumes at their banquets and festivals. The floors of the rooms were strewn with flowers, and fragrant petals were scattered on the guests from the velarium that stretched across the ceiling of the apartment.

In the city of Rome in particular, the cult of

82

perfumes, especially in connexion with the rose, was carried to an extravagant extent and apparently became a craze. When dining, the wealthy nobles delighted to have fountains playing with rose-water, rose leaves were scattered on the floors of

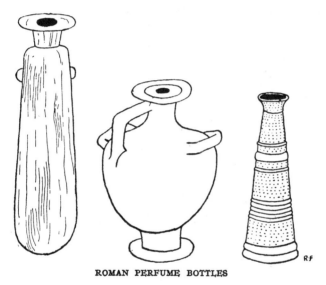

ROMAN PERFUME BOTTLES

the apartments or showered upon the heads of the guests from above, while garlands were placed on their brows and festooned over their robes.

Heliogabalus is said to have carried his love for roses still further, and drank a wine of roses and even bathed in the fragrant liquid. Roses were

83

part of his food and drink, and when he was taken ill, he demanded that in his medicine roses should form a prominent ingredient.

Cosmetics and powders for the skin were very frequently used by Roman women. These sometimes took the form of pastes made of pea-flour or barley-meal, which were applied to the skin and allowed to remain for several hours, in order to make it soft and supple.

Juvenal thus alludes to the prevailing fashion for cosmetics in his time:

Th' eclipse then vanishes; and all her face
Is opened and restored to every grace;
The crust removed, her cheeks as smooth as silk
Are polished with a wash of asses' milk.

Poppæa, the wife of Nero, is said to have set the fashion of bathing in asses' milk every day, and when she was exiled from Rome she took fifty of these animals with her, so she might have a plentiful supply. It is thus mentioned by a Roman writer:

And should she to the farthest north be sent,
A train of these attend her banishment.

Ovid, in a fragment of a book that has come down to us, gives the following advice to women on how to beautify their complexions: "Learn from me the art of imparting to your complexion a dazzling whiteness. Divest from its husk the barley brought by our own vessels from the Libyan fields. Take two pounds of this barley with an equal quantity of bean-flour, and mix them with ten eggs. When these have been dried in the air, have them ground and add the sixth part of a pound of hartshorn. When the whole has been reduced to a fine flour, pass it through a sieve, and complete the preparation with twelve narcissus bulbs that have been pounded in a mortar, two ounces of gum, as much Tuscan-seed, and eighteen ounces of honey. Every woman who spreads this paste on her face will render it smoother and more brilliant than her mirror."

For removing blotches from the skin he recommends a mixture of roasted lupins, beans, white lead, red nitre, and orris root made into a paste with Attic honey.

In connexion with this recipe, it is interesting to recall that the women of ancient Egypt used powdered lupin seeds with water to wash the skin.

For colouring the face, Roman women used white lead or chalk, a red colouring matter called fucus for the cheeks, and Egyptian kohl for darkening the eyes.

85

In alluding to the custom of presenting the guests at a banquet with perfumed unguents, Martial, in his " Epigrams," says: " I admit, Fabullus, that you gave a good ointment to your guests yesterday, but there was a lack of carving. It is a ridiculous thing to be well perfumed and to starve."

The quality of the meal as compared to the perfume is again mentioned in the following lines,

Faith, your essence was excelling,
But you gave us nought to eat;
Nothing tasting, sweetly smelling
Is, Fabullus, scarce a treat.

Catullus has an invitation to a feast in which he is promised " rare essences," on which he remarks:

Thou'lt pray the gods may touch and taste
Be quite in smell alone effaced,
And I become all Nose.
Balm delights me; it is the perfume for men.
Ye matrons scent yourselves with the essence of Cosmus.

The Romans had a maxim, " Never think of leaving perfumes or wine to your heir. Administer these yourself and let him have your money."

During the games in the amphitheatres the whole air is said to have been filled with the odours that arose from the burning censers that were placed around the arena.

The most popular perfume among the Romans was probably the Sweet-smelling Rush, while the Roses of Pæstum, Spikenard, Onegalium, Medebathrim, Balm of Gilead, and Cinnamon were also held in high esteem.

Extravagance in the use of perfumes was eventually carried to such an extent that, under the Consulate of Licinius Crassus, a law was passed restricting the use of perfumery, on the grounds that it might cause a shortage of the fragrant materials employed in the ceremonies in the temples.

After the fall of the Empire, the use of perfumes waned considerably among the Romans, but the love of sweet odours still survives with the Italians to-day. Their flowers fill the air with fragrance and their churches are redolent with the scent of the incense.

CHAPTER IX

THE importation of the fragrant gums from Arabia and the East, which were generally known as spices in the Middle Ages, was an essential factor in the development of the art of perfumery. The first body which appears to have dealt in these substances in England was the Guild of Pepperers of London, who are mentioned in the Pipe Rolls as early as 1179. They were a company of traders or merchants who imported medicinal and other kinds of spices together with drugs from the shores of the Red Sea and various Eastern ports. Some time after the formation of the Guild they amalgamated with another body called the Spicers, who traded in similar wares, but they ultimately fell into difficulties and a new fraternity of Pepperers was founded. In London they were known as the Pepperers or Easterlings of Soper's Lane and the Spicers of the Ward of Chepe, from the districts in which they carried on their business, where they had stalls or shops for the sale of perfumes, spices, and drugs. They paid a toll of a certain quantity of pepper to the King each year.

A large number of the spicers were Italians, while the Easterlings were chiefly Germans from the Baltic coast and the Hanse towns, who brought spices from the East and placed them on the English market through the Pepperers and Spicers, who thus became the distributors.

St. Anthony was their patron saint, and until the year 1373 they bore the title of the Fraternity of St. Anthony.

According to their ordinances in 1376 " no one of other mistery shall be admitted into the company without the common consent." A spirit of jealousy, however, grew up between the two branches, and as years went on the breach became wider, the brotherly love and unity of the promoters evidently became a dead-letter, and the title of Fraternity of St. Anthony was dropped and that of the Company of Grocers substituted, to which Henry VI granted a charter in 1428.

There seems little doubt that the Pepperers, Spicers, and Apothecaries were originally branches of the same trade, the latter dealing more in drugs for medicinal use, and the former in the spices and aromatic gums exported from the East through Italy to this country.

In our cities in the thirteenth century certain traders appear to have congregated in particular localities, and in the markets their stalls were often placed together, as they sometimes are to-day. Each craft or guild had its own place assigned to it for the convenience of traffic and the adjustment of prices by the guildsmen themselves.

Thus we find records of districts in some towns called the Spicery. There was one in Oxford in the parish of All Saints. In 1313 there is record of one Odin the Spicer, who was an official at the Court of Edward II, and received sevenpence halfpenny a day as apothecary to the Queen.

In the fifteenth century the London Spicers centred in Bucklersbury, their stalls and booths being erected there, and for centuries the district has been associated with them. As recently as 1878 an old firm of druggists carried on their business in the street. Falstaff, alluding to the young gallants of his time " that they smell like Bucklersbury in simple time," evidently referred to the bundles of freshly gathered herbs that were hung up to dry over the stalls or from the ceilings of the shops.

Kingsley, in " Westward Ho! " makes Mrs. Tenterhook exclaim, " Go into Bucklersbury and fetch me two ounces of preserved melounes; look

90

that there be no tobacco taken at the shop when he weighs it."

From the Spicers, the trade appears to have passed into the hands of the Apothecaries, and although the use of perfumes came into vogue in England in Tudor times, they were at first mostly brought from France and Italy. There seems to be no record of a perfumer in London until the seventeenth or early eighteenth century, when Charles Lilly kept a shop in the Strand where he prepared and sold " snuffs and perfumes which refresh the brain in those that have too much for their quiet, and gladdens it in those who have too little to know the want of it."

It is not generally known that the embalming of the body with spices was practised in England in Tudor times. In the funeral expenses of Sir Edward Darrell, who died at Littlecote in 1549, the sum of 37 shillings is charged for " spice for bawminge of his corse."

The chemists, who were partly an off-shoot of the apothecaries, began to open shops in the seventeenth century. They distilled the aromatic waters like lavender, elderflower, and rosemary, which were so much esteemed at that period, and sold hair-lotions and powders for the teeth. Up to this time most ladies of quality kept their own books of recipes for all kinds of domestic medicines and perfumes, which they prepared in their still-rooms, and with these we shall deal later.

The alchemists also played a part in the development of perfumery from mediæval times, and sought the extraction of odours from flowers and regarded perfumes as of great importance in their work.

Thomas Norton, an alchemist of Bristol, who wrote a remarkable work, called the " Ordinall of Alkimy," in 1447, tells of the value of odours in his investigations in the following quaint passages:

When substance shall putrifie,
Horrible odors are engendered thereby
as of dragons, and of men that long dead be,
their stinke may cause much mortalitie.
It is not holsome to smell to some soules
for quenching some snuff a mare will cast her foals.
Fishes love sweete smells also it is true
they love not old kettles as they doe newe.
all things that is of good odor hath naturall heate
though Camphir, Roses and thinges cold
have sweet odors as Authors have soules.
No good odor is contrary to another but it is so of
    stinkinge smelle
For stinke of garlic avoideth stinke of dunghill.
Of odors this doctrine is sufficient

92

as in alchemie to serve your intent.
Your workes to understand thereby,
When things begin to putrifie.
Also by odors this maie you learne,
Subtilness and groseness of matters to discerne.
A sweete-smelling thinge hath more puritie
and more of spirituall than stinkinge maie bee.
As colours changeth in your sight
So odors changeth the smelling by might.
The cause of odors to know if you delight
Four things there to be requisite.
First, that subtill matter be obedient to the working
    of heate.
The working of heate as it sheweth in Stone,
Heate maketh odors into stinkinge, by reason,
Dung hills in sommer
stinke more than winter season.
Pleasant odors ingendered be shall
Of cleare and pure substance fumigall,
As it appeareth in Amber, Nard and Myrtle.
Good for a woman for such thinges please her,
But of pure substance with a meane in heatte
Be temperate odors, as in violett.
Of meane heate, with substance impure
is odor unpleaynge, as Aloes and Sulphur.

The alchemists relied upon certain odours to
reveal the results of their experiments, just as the

pharmacist is trained to recognise preparations of drugs by their smell. Thus Norton continues:

Ye will by smelling learne
Of ye principall agent trulie to declare,
As white and black be colours in extremitie,
So of odors sweet and stinkinge there bee,
But where that slighted know by sight,
Mean colours show that ye maie be aright.
So meane odors shall not by smellinge
Be known of you, that is the cause why
The nostrils be open as in the fishe's eye.

It is chiefly from the experiments and observations made by these early workers in science that the basis of the perfumer's art was formed.

CHAPTER X

THE art of perfumery began to be cultivated in Italy early in the sixteenth century, when Venice became the centre for the trade in aromatic gums and sweet-smelling woods, brought to that city from Constantinople and the East by the ships of the merchants.

A demand arose from the princes and nobles, who at this time began to use perfumes largely in their palaces in the city of the Doges.

The monks, who had long cultivated flowers and plants in the monastic gardens and knew something of botany and chemistry, appear to have been the first to supply the demand.

The fashion soon spread south to Florence, for as early as 1508 a laboratory for the manufacture of perfumes was founded in the monastery of Santa Maria Novella in that city. It was established by the Dominicans, who, like most of the monastic orders, were skilled in the medicinal use of herbs.

95

Each director is said to have set himself out to devise some new recipe to add to the fame of the order, and so the preparations made in the monastery became celebrated, not only throughout Italy, but also in other countries.

Fra Angiolo Paladini originated several applications for the skin and devised an almond paste, a lily-water, and a cosmetic vinegar which achieved renown among the ladies of the Tuscan Court. Fra Cavalieri invented a Cinchona Elixir in 1659 which was highly valued for fevers. Another director, Fra Ludivico Berlingacci, in 1707, discovered and made his famous " Life Elixir "; and Pope Innocent XI presented the Order with a wonderful recipe for burns which became known as " Balsam Innocenziano."

During the seventeenth and eighteenth centuries the laboratory became well known for its scents, which were placed in tiny bottles in small boxes or cases, often in the shape of a book, the cover being stamped with ornamental devices in gold or colour.

In one of the recently published " Pepys letters," from his nephew John Jackson, who was making the grand tour in Italy, there is an allusion to one of these little cases in the form of a book. Among the articles he sent his uncle from Leghorn he men-

tions " one small book of Florence essences,"
which there is little doubt was one of the products
of the Santa Maria Novella laboratory. He also
alludes to " a franchepan ball," probably a preparation of the famous Frangipani perfume that was
then so much used in Rome, and a " small paper
of pastilles to burn for fumigation," which were at
that time evidently a curiosity.

The story of the origin of the perfume known
as Frangipani is an interesting one. The formula
is said to have been first devised by a Roman noble-
man, a member of the Frangipani family, whose
name is said to have been derived from an office
performed by its members, who had the right to
supply the wafer or bread to the Church for sacra-
mental purposes. Originally the perfume was in
the form of a dry powder and was used in little
bags or in a soft mass for the cassolette. The liquid
scent is said to have been first made by Mercutio
Frangipani, a grandson of the inventor, who found
that by digesting the dry ingredients in spirit of
wine he obtained a more lasting perfume. It is
stated that he was a learned student of botany and
accompanied Columbus on his voyage to the West
Indies. It was he who told his fellow-voyagers
that the perfume which was wafted to them on
approaching the Island of Antigua came from the

H

flowers, which they found in great quantities. The Plumiera alba, which has a very powerful odour, was among them, and the inhabitants of the island still call it the Frangipani flower.

Another member of the family served in the Papal Army in France in the reign of Charles IX, and to his grandson, the Marquis Frangipani, is attributed a process for perfuming gloves, known as Frangipani gloves, which became fashionable at that time.

In connexion with Italy, mention should be made of the " Golden Rose," the special gift of the Popes to royal personages or distinguished women, as the highest mark of their esteem. It is said to have originally taken the form of the model of a single flower in gold, but in more recent times it has been made in the shape of a small tree with several flowers, mounted on a golden stand. It is sometimes richly ornamented and studded with precious stones, and the flowers are perfumed with ambergris, musk, and other aromatics.

Before the fifteenth century it was simply anointed with balsam and perfumed with musk, the thorns and the petals being tinged red to symbolize the Passion, but latterly the " Golden Rose " has been blessed by the Pope each year with a certain ritual. After this he takes it in his left hand and

98

blesses the people, and this is followed by the celebration of Mass in the Sistine Chapel.

King Henry VIII received the " Golden Rose " from Pope Clement; in 1861 it was awarded to the Queen of Spain; and in 1862 it was given to the Empress of the French.

France has been associated with the cultivation of sweet-smelling flowers from early times, and there is a tradition that the Romans imported and obtained many of their perfumes from ancient Gaul. It was customary with them to place perfume boxes with the dead, but it was not until the time of Francis I and Catharine de' Medici that perfumery may be said to have become an art.

As early as 1190 there is record that there were makers and sellers of perfumes in Paris, and under Colbert the perfumers obtained patents registered in Parliament, and their fraternity was established at St. Anne's Chapel in the Church of the Innocents.

By patents granted by King Henry VI of England and France in 1426 the arms of the perfumers were registered in the Armorial General of France. They are interesting as showing their connexion with the art of perfuming gloves, and

99

are represented by three red gloves and a gold perfume box or cassolette.

Catharine de' Medici brought among her entourage from Italy, Cosmo Ruggiero, her astrologer and alchemist, who is said to have made her essences, perfumes, and powders. He had an apartment allotted to him in the Tuileries which was connected with those of the Queen by a secret staircase. She also had in her train a Florentine named René, who was expert in the art of making perfumes. He opened a shop in Paris which soon became the meeting-place of the fashionable world of the period. His scents and cosmetics speedily became famous and were used by all the beauties of the Court.

Dumas gives an interesting and picturesque description of the shop of René at the close of the sixteenth century. He says:

" In the midst of the houses which bordered the line of the Pont-Saint-Michel, facing a small islet, was a house remarkable for its panels of wood, over which a large roof impended. The low façade was painted blue with rich gold mouldings, and a kind of frieze, which separated the ground from the first floor, represented groups of devils in the most grotesque postures imaginable. It was in the shop on the ground-floor that there was the

100

RENÉ'S SHOP IN PARIS—SIXTEENTH CENTURY

daily sale of perfumery, unguents, cosmetics, and all the articles of a skilful chemist.

" In the shop, which was large and deep, there were two doors, each leading to a staircase. Both led to a room on the first floor, which was divided by tapestry suspended in the centre, in the back portion of which was a door leading to a secret staircase. Another door opened to a small chamber, lighted from the roof, which contained a large stove, alembics, retorts, and crucibles; it was an alchemist's laboratory.

" In the front portion of the room on the first floor were Ibises of Egypt; mummies with gilded bands; the crocodile yawning from the ceiling; death's heads with eyeless sockets and gumless teeth, and here old musty volumes, torn and rat-eaten, were presented to the eye of the visitor in pell-mell confusion. Behind the curtain were phials, singularly-shaped boxes and vases of curious construction; all lighted up by two silver lamps which, supplied with perfumed oil, cast their yellow flame around the sombre vault, to which each was suspended by three blackened chains."

A romantic story is related of the tragic end of the beautiful Gabrielle d'Estrées when she was sent by Henry IV from Fontainebleau to Paris.

He had arranged for her to go to the house of Zametti, an Italian Jew, who had originally come to France in the household of Catharine de' Medici and had become chief money-lender to the King. He lived in great style in a magnificently furnished palace near the Arsénal.

Although reluctant to go to Zametti, as if she had a premonition of evil, after a tender farewell from the King, Gabrielle embarked in a royal barge, which was attended by a flotilla of boats decorated with flags and streamers in the Venetian style.

On arrival in Paris, she was met on the quay by Zametti and a number of nobles and attendants, who escorted her to her lodging.

After sleeping the night, she arose early to attend Mass in a church close by, but before leaving the palace, Zametti presented her with an exquisitely decorated scent-bottle containing a strong perfume. During the service she fainted, and was carried back to the palace and placed at her own wish in the garden.

Another fainting attack followed, from which she was revived with difficulty. When she recovered, she ordered a litter to be instantly prepared, in which she was borne to the house of her aunt near the Louvre. Here she was put to bed

103

and " lay with her eyes opened and turned upward, her face livid and her mouth distorted." She called constantly for the King, but was too ill to write to him.

She was shortly seized with convulsions and died soon afterwards, it was believed poisoned by the perfume in the filigree scent-bottle, or by means of some food of which she had partaken while at the palace of Zametti.

Thus ended the romantic life of Gabrielle d'Estrées, but whether her death was due to the perfume or to natural causes we shall never know.

In 1548 the authorities of the city of Paris paid six golden crowns to one Georges Marteau for herbs and plants to perfume the public fountains on the occasion of a festival.

During the reign of Henry III the popularity of perfumes had so increased that in 1582 we find Nicolas de Montant reproving the women for using " all sorts of perfumes, cordial waters, civet, musk, ambergris, and other precious aromatics to perfume their clothes and linen, and even their whole bodies."

Diana of Poitiers was one of the leading patronesses of perfumes and cosmetics of her time, and attributed the preservation of her beauty to

104

their aid, and so was able to outshine all her rivals.

During the time of the Valois the use of perfumes among the higher class increased, but afterwards it appears to have waned until Louis XIII and Anne of Austria came to the throne, when the fashionable world again veered round in their favour.

Although Louis XIV is said to have discouraged their use at Court, according to Fournier, he had a great love for perfumes, and is described by him as "the sweetest-smelling monarch that he had ever seen." He used to receive Martial, his perfumer, in his private closet to compose the odours he employed on his sacred person.

It was customary at that time for persons of rank and fashion to superintend the making of the special perfumes they favoured; thus the Prince of Condé always had his favourite snuff scented in his presence.

The names of distinguished people were often associated with both perfumes and cosmetics; thus the celebrated Poudre à la Maréchale, which was introduced about this time, took its name from Madame la Maréchale d'Aumont, who is said to have originated it.

During the Regency all the Court beauties used

105

perfumes lavishly. Ninon de Lenclos claimed to have preserved her beauty until her sixtieth year by the aid of the wonderful cosmetics she constantly used, and the Du Barry, whose appearance suggested perennial youth, was said to have obtained the secret recipes for her toilet preparations from the notorious Cagliostro.

In the time of Louis XV the use of perfumery grew still more fashionable, and it became customary with the habitués of the Court at Versailles, which was called " la Cour parfumée," to use a different perfume every day.

Richelieu was a firm believer in the revivifying power of perfumes, and during his last illness insisted on sweet-smelling powders being diffused in his room by means of a bellows.

The household expenses of Madame de Pompadour at Choisy show her fondness for perfumes, the bills for which at one time amounted to 500,000 livres a year.

Marie Antoinette is said to have set the fashion in using the perfumes of violet and rose, which she preferred to the more powerful odours usually affected before her time.

The use of the perfumed bath, which Voltaire terms the " luxury of luxuries," was revived towards the end of the eighteenth century. Madame

A PERFUMER'S SHOP
(From an engraving of the seventeenth century.)

107

Tallien favoured a bath of crushed strawberries and raspberries, after which she was gently rubbed with sponges soaked in perfumed milk.

The art of perfumery in France began to be studied scientifically towards the end of the seventeenth century, and the first work treating the subject from this point of view was published by Liebault in 1628.

Flowers began to be specially cultivated for the purpose of extracting their sweet odours, and the sun-warmed hills of the Var commenced to be famous for the production of the delicate and fragrant perfumes which are now known throughout the world.

CHAPTER XI

THE FRENCH GLOVE PERFUMERS

GLOVE making in France is an industry of some antiquity, and as early as 1190 statutes were passed regulating the craft by Philip Augustus. The art of perfuming gloves began to be practised early in the sixteenth century, and was carried on by the merchants, masters, and glove perfumers who obtained the right to make them and also to sell perfumes.

The perfumed skins, which were impregnated with ambergris, musk, or civet, were imported from Italy and Spain for making the gloves and other articles.

The substances employed were first mixed with a fatty basis, and then smeared on the inside of the gloves with the further object of keeping the skin soft.

In a manuscript written in the latter part of the sixteenth century, the following recipe for the perfume is given:

" To perfume a pair of gloves for ye King's most ' excell ' Majesty.

" Take two ounces of oil of sweet almonds, 3 ozs. of Storax, and roots of white lilies, and finely powder and mingle with oyle. Leave them for six days. Wash the gloves very well in fair water and dry well. Then dip them in Rose water, and let them dry in the shadow, then wipe them with the oyle and let them dry."

Perfumed gloves appear to have come into use in England about 1550. Stow records that " Milloners or haberdashers had not then any gloves imbroyered or trimmed with gold or silke; neither could they make any costly wash or perfume, until about the fifteenth year of the Queen [Elizabeth] when the Right Honourable Edwarde de Vere, Earl of Oxford, came from Italy, and brought with him, gloves, sweet bags, a perfumed leather jerkin and other pleasant things; and that year the Queen had a pair of perfumed gloves trimmed only with four tuffes or roses of coloured silks; the Queen took such pleasure in those gloves, that she was pictured with those gloves upon her hands, and for many years after it was called the Earl of Oxford's perfume."

A general liking for perfumes appears to have been manifested in England in Elizabethan times. The Queen herself had a particular fondness for them, and she is said to have had an extremely

keen sense of smell. " Perfumes," says a writer
in the Tudor period, " were never richer, more
elaborate, more costly or more delicate than in
Elizabeth's reign."

The Queen expressed great delight with the
gifts of the perfume boxes which she received from
time to time, and the ladies of the Court used perfumes in great quantities.

Coffers of cedar or sweet-smelling sandal-wood
usually formed part of the furniture in the bed-
rooms, for the purpose of keeping linen and
clothes. Scent, or " casting bottles," as they were
called at that time, used for sprinkling perfumed
waters for the toilet, were to be found in every
lady's chamber.

The Queen had a cloak of Spanish perfumed
leather, and her shoes were also scented with
sweet essences.

The still-room formed a part of every castle
and country house, where the aromatic waters, conserves, and remedies for domestic use were prepared from the recipe book which was kept by
every housewife. Nichols says that at Hawkstead,
" the Queen had a still-room where ladies of the
Court amused themselves in distilling fragrant
waters."

In connexion with Queen Elizabeth's love for

perfumes, there is an interesting letter preserved among the Lansdown MSS., from one Ralph Rabbards to the Queen.

The writer, who edited Ripley's " Compound of Alchemy " in 1591, describes himself as a " gentleman studious and expert in Archemical Artes," and says that he sends her Majestie some notes on some " moste pleasant serviceable and rare inventions, as I have by long studdie and chargeable practice founde out, and am ready to put in execution at a smalle charge."

Among these he mentions " waters of purest substance from odors, flowers, fruites and herbes wholsomest, perfitest and of greatest vertue are first distilled by desensory, depured and rectified, clere as crystall, with his owne onlie proper vertue, taste and odor contynuinge many years. One spoonfull is better than a gallon for any prynce or noble person, or any that love their healthe; for medecyne inward or outward, where other doe much more hurte than good, being inaptly distilled and invenomed by the evill quallitie of mettalyne stilles."

Rabbards, however, does not reveal the secret of his discovery, but proceeds to extol his " water for odors moste sweete and delicate of many severall kyndes. Water of violetts, and suche

112

like water of violetts, jilly-flowers and pinckes, etc., contynue not to reteyne their owne proper odors and vertues, except they be distilled very cunningly and perfitly by desensory, or their odors beinge helpen by other meanes."

Finally, he recommends his "waters to clense and keepe brighte the skynne and fleshe and preserve it in his perfitt state."

CHAPTER XII

PRIOR to the sixteenth century there are but few records of the perfumes used in England.

It is stated that when Hugh the Great, father of Hugh Capet, sent to ask the hand of the sister of King Athelstan in marriage, he gave as presents " such perfumes as had never been seen in England."

Charlemagne also is said to have been very fond of perfumes, and they were much in favour at his Court at Aix-la-Chapelle.

The perfumes chiefly used in the sixteenth century were generally in the form of dry powders, or the flower petals were mixed with certain crushed aromatic gums and powdered roots, as in a pot-pourri. The perfumed waters were distilled from the flowers with water, and the use of spirit of wine or alcohol for extracting the essential oil was practically unknown.

A favourite odour at this period appears to have

been the damask rose, and in the manuscript recipe books of the time many formulæ are to be found for making the "Damask Powder." Here is one that dates from 1563: "Take leaves from the Damask rose and mix with Musk, Storax, Labdanum, Gum benzoin, Gallingal and Calamus, and you will have a fine odor."

These dry perfumes were sometimes placed in little silk bags, so that they could be conveniently carried in the pocket or placed among clothes.

The following recipes, from a manuscript of the sixteenth century, show the composition of some of these old perfumes:

"To make swete powder for Bagges. Take Damask rose leaves, orris root, calaminth, benzoin gum, and make into a powder and fill ye bagges."

Another consists of "Powders of Callamus, Orris, Roses, White Sanders [sandal-wood], Benimyn [benzoin], Cypres, Violetts and Spyke. Mingle together."

One of the earliest recipes for Lavender-water perfume occurs in a French manuscript book of the seventeenth century, although the simple water distilled from the flowers with water was prepared in the still-rooms of England long before that period. It was employed as a medicine as well as a perfume.

" A violette Powder for the perfuming of linen used by the King Henry of France " is included in this book of recipes. It consists of " Orris root, rose leaves, santal wood, cypres, benjamen, marjoleine, storax, calamus, giroffle, ambergris, coriander and lavender." These were to be made into a powder, mixed together dry, and made into sachets.

Chipre, or Chypre, was a favourite odour in France at that time and is largely used to-day. In the seventeenth century, it was composed of benzoin, storax, calaminth, calamus root, and coriander, mixed together and used in the form of a dry powder.

Another recipe for making it, culled from a manuscript of the seventeenth century, is as follows:

" To make ye powder of Red Chypre. Take, Damask Roses 2 ozs., Red Santal wood 1 oz., Aloes wood $\frac{1}{4}$ oz., Giroffle 30 grs., Musk 12 grs., Ambergris 8 grs., Civet 8 grs. Powder and well mix together."

Ladies of rank took a pride in collecting recipes and adding them to their manuscript books, which were greatly valued and usually preserved with care, and handed down from one generation to another. They generally included recipes for

116

cookery, confections, perfumes, conserves, cordial waters, domestic medicines and others that could be prepared in the still-room.

Among a French collection dated 1631, in the British Museum, is an interesting recipe for a sachet powder used by Queen Isabella of Spain. To make this celebrated " Sachet Powder," it is directed to take, " rose leaves, orris root, calamus, storax, benzoin, girofle flowers, and coriander, and rub them to powder, then mix them with great care."

In another manuscript of the late sixteenth century is a recipe for " a Paste for the Casolette " used by the Duchess of Braganza and the Duchess of Parma. It was composed of " Ambergris 3 drachms, musk 2 drachms, civette 1 drachm, oil of giroffle 1 drachm, essence of citron 3 drachms. Mix the ambergris, musk, and civet together, then add the oil and essence and make the whole into a paste with rose-water and place in the casolette."

The cassolette, or printanier, was a little box generally made of ivory, silver, or gold, with a lid perforated with holes, which could be held to the nose and its fragrant contents inhaled. They were sometimes beautifully decorated and jewelled, and often carried by ladies of fashion.

The perfumes used varied according to the

117

taste of the owner. The perfume for gloves for the Duchess, was made with ambergris, musk, oil of jasmine, and rose-water, with which they were to be well rubbed. Another and more elaborate perfume, in which gloves were to be saturated and then allowed to dry, consisted of " Roses 1 lb., Orris 1 lb., Benzoin ½ oz., Storax ½ oz., Calamus 6 ozs., Essence of Citron 3 ozs., Coriander ½ oz., Girofle 6 ozs., Lavender ¼ oz., Powder of Orange ½ oz., Rose wood 4 ozs., Santal ½ oz., Demy Muscade."

" The Perfume Necklace to be worn by ladies " is directed to be made as follows: Take " 1 ounce of Benjamin, 1 ounce of Storax and 1 ounce of Labdanum. Heat in a mortar very hot, and beat all these gums to a perfect paste; in beating of it, put in 6 grains of Musk, 4 grains of Civet. When you have beaten all this to a fine paste, with your hands with rose water, roll it round betwixt your hands, and make holes in the beads, and so string them while they be hot."

Finger-rings for holding a few grains of dry perfume came into use at a later period. In the centre of the bezel was a little box, the hinged cover of which was pierced with tiny holes, so that the contents could be smelt by the wearer when placed to the nose.

118

During the sixteenth and seventeenth centuries many books were written, especially by Italians, which were said to contain secret recipes in great variety, for which there was evidently a considerable demand.

One of the most popular of these, which passed through many editions, was "The Secrets of Alexis," first printed about 1555, and afterwards translated into several languages. It is said to have been compiled by Girolamo Ruscelli, who adopted the pseudonym of "Master Alexis of Piedmont," and contains some curious recipes, including one for making the "oile of Redde Dog," as well as several for perfumes used at that period.

His formula for "Damask Perfume" consists of: musk, 5 grains; civet, 2 grains; ambergris, 4 grains; fine sugar, 4 grains; benzoin, 1 grain; storax, 3 grains; calamus, 3 grains; aloes-wood, 2 grains. "Beat them well into powder, and put together in a little perfume-pan. Pour it into as much Rose water as will be two fingers high, and make under it a small fire that it may not boil, and when the water is consumed, you shall pour in another and continue this doing a certaine number of days."

He also gives a recipe to make "little cushions of perfumed roses," and a "perfume for the chamber." The latter was to be made and used as follows:

Take of "Storax, Calamint, Benzoin, Aloes wood, of each one ounce, Coales [ashes] of Willow, well beaten into powder, five ounces. These things mixed with Aqua Vitæ, as much as will make a paste. Make thereof little cakes, or other forms if you will, and so keep them. And when you will use or occupy it, put it into a fire, for in consuming little and little, it will make a singular good odour in the place where you burn it."

Another way of diffusing odours in a room was the perfume lamp, and a recipe is given for making a powder of aromatic gums, which is to be put into a little pan and placed over a lamp so that the smoke may fill the apartment with a "swete odour."

"A very good perfume for to trim gloves with little cost and yet will continue long" is given at great length. It was necessary that "the gloves should be of good thick leather."

Civet was a favourite perfume for gloves, and there is a recipe for "a very excellent Civet to perfume gloves and to anoint a mans handes with."

Another method recommended to make "an excellent perfume to perfume chambers, garments, coverlets, sheets and all other things belonging to

any Prince," is to " take citron-peel and civet, and
heat them on some coals in the midst of the
chamber, much better if you add musk and
ambergris." For linen, the ingredients are to be
made into pills or balls and placed in a coffer with
it.

To make " a verie good perfume against the
Plague," says Master Alexis, " you must take Mas-
tich, Chypre, Incense, Mace, Wormwood, Myrrh,
Aloes wood, Musk, Ambergris, Nutmegs, Myrtle,
Bay, Rosemary, Sage, Roses, Elder, Cloves, Juniper, Rue and Pitch. All these things stamped and
mixed together, you shall set upon the coales and
so perfume the Chamber."

During the Stuart period the perfumed bath
came into vogue among women of fashion in
England. A favourite recipe for " A sweet-scented
Bath " was as follows: Take of " Roses, Citron
flowers, Orange flowers, Jasmine, Bays, Rosemary,
Lavender, Mint, Pennyroyal and Citron peel, each
a sufficient quantity, boyl them together gently, and
make a bath, to which add Oyl of Spike 6 drops,
Musk 5 grains, Ambergrease 3 grains, sweet Asa
1 ounce. Let her go into the Bath before meat."

The Court beauties of Charles II's time had a
fondness for a perfume composed of ambergris,
musk, and sandal-wood, which were powdered,

mixed together, and placed in small bags that could be worn on the person, or put among their clothes in the oak chests and coffers, the usual receptacles for apparel found in most houses of the period.

Lavender, which was plentiful and largely grown in the country, was the favourite odour for linen, and was kept in the presses, not only for imparting its perfume, but also to prevent the ravages of moths.

" Let's go to that house," says Izaak Walton, " for the linen looks white and smells of lavender and I long to be in a pair of sheets that smell so."

CHAPTER XIII

PERFUMES OF SHAKESPEARE'S TIME

ALTHOUGH Shakespeare makes frequent mention in his plays of the beauty of flowers and their fragrance, there are but few allusions to the perfumes which were in use in his time.

The rose, pre-eminent among flowers for its beauty and perfume, was evidently a favourite with the poet, and he often alludes to it in the " Sonnets," as instanced in the lines:

The rose looks fair, but fairer we it deem
For that sweet odour which doth in it live.
The canker-blooms have full as deep a dye
As the perfumed tincture of the roses,
Hang on such thorns and play as wantonly
When summer's breath their masked buds discloses:
But, for their virtue only is their show,
They live unwoo'd and unrespected fade;
Die to themselves. Sweet roses do not so;
Of their sweet deaths are sweetest odours made.

The violet, the lily, and marjoram are also mentioned in later stanzas, thus:

Nor the sweet smell
Of different flowers in odour and in hue
Could make me any summer's story tell,
Or from their proud lap pluck them where they grew;
Nor did I wonder at the lily's white,
Nor praise the deep vermilion in the rose.

The forward violet thus did I chide:
Sweet thief, whence did thou steal thy sweet that smells,
If not from my love's breath?   The purple pride
Which on thy soft cheek for complexion dwells
In my love's veins thou hast too grossly dy'd.
The lily I condemned for thy hand,
And buds of marjoram had stol'n thy hair:
The roses fearfully on thorns did stand,
One blushing shame, another white despair;
A third, nor red nor white, had stol'n of both,
And to his robbery had annex'd thy breath.

In "The Taming of the Shrew" there is an allusion to Rose-water for perfuming the hands:

What is it your honour will command?
Let one attend him with a silver basin
Full of rose water, and bestrew'd with flowers.

In " Much Ado about Nothing," alluding to Benedict, Pedro says:

Nay, he rubs himself with civet;
Can you smell him out by that?

And in the " Merry Wives of Windsor," Mrs. Quickly, when telling Falstaff of all the presents made to Mistress Ford, exclaims:

Letter after letter, gift after gift,
Smelling so sweetly, all of musk.

In " What You Will," Marston says:

Now are the lawn sheets fumed with violets,

probably alluding to the use of the perfume-pan; while in " Much Ado about Nothing," Borachio speaks of " being entertained for a perfumer as I was smoking a musty room."

The perfume-pan was employed to fumigate and perfume apartments that had been closed, and also for imparting a sweet smell to linen and clothes. Strype, writing in 1549, states that Sir J. Cheke " sent for a perfume-pan for his apartment."

The perfumed gloves so often used in the six-

teenth century are mentioned by Autolycus in
" The Winter's Tale " as follows:

Gloves as sweet as damask roses;
Masks for faces and for noses;
Bugle bracelet, necklace amber,
Perfume for a lady's chamber.

For sprinkling perfume on the head, face, and
hands in Shakespeare's time, a vessel called a
" casting bottle," with a top or stopper pierced with
little holes, was generally used. An allusion to
it is made by Marston in " Antonio and Mallida."
In one scene, a young gallant enters with a
" casting bottle " of sweet water in his hand,
sprinkling himself, remarking, " as sweet and
neat as a barber's ' casting bottle ' " ; and in
Ford's play " The Fairies," one of the characters
is discovered sprinkling his hair and face with
scented water from a " casting bottle."

In the sixteenth century it was customary in
houses of the better class to strew the floors with
sweet rushes, and in the churches, the pews occu-
pied by the gentlefolk were sometimes similarly
strewn with flowers.

In the play " Apius and Virginia," one of the
characters thus alludes to the custom:—

126

Thou knave, but for thee ere this time of day,
My lady's fair pew had been strewn full gay
With primroses, cowslips and violets sweet,
With mints and with marygold and marjoram meet,
Which now lyeth uncleanly and all along of thee.

In Spain and Portugal the custom of strewing the floors with lavender and rosemary survived until recent years.

Burton, in his "Anatomy of Melancholy," states that "the smoke of Juniper is in great request with us to sweeten our chambers"; and Ben Jonson alludes to it in the lines: "He doth sacrifice twopence to her every morning before she rises, to sweeten the room by burning it."

In France, "perfume bellows" were often employed to diffuse sweet-smelling powders throughout an apartment, and Cardinal Richelieu is said to have been especially fond of having his room perfumed in this manner.

In the time of the Commonwealth the use of perfumes in England much decreased, and, like other articles of luxury, they were discouraged by the Puritans; but with the Restoration they again came into fashion, with paint, powder, and patches, among the higher class. Hair-powder, which came in with the wigs, was used at a later period, and has continued to some extent to the present day, for its use still survives in the powdered hair customary for footmen.

In the early eighteenth century the travelling perfume-seller, like the quack doctor, frequented the market-places and fairs in country towns and villages, and we owe to Shadwell, who was Poet Laureate in 1676, an interesting description of one of these itinerant vendors of sweet odours, which he gives in his play " Virtuoso ":

" I have choice good gloves, Amber, Orangery, Genoa, Romane, Frangepane, Neroly, Tuberose, Jessamine and Marshall; all manner of tires for the head, locks, tours, frowzes, combs and so forth; all manner of waters, almond water and mercury for the complexion and the best pomatums of Europe, but a rare one made of lamb's caul and May dew; also all manner of confections of mercury and hog's bones to preserve present and to restore lost beauty."

This is reminiscent of a recipe given by Master Alexis for a " Water to make women beautiful for ever," which was prepared by taking " a young raven from the nest, feeding it on hard boiled eggs for forty days, then after killing it, distilling it with myrtle leaves, talc and almond oil."

From time to time in reading historical narra-

128

A TRAVELLING PERFUME-SELLER IN THE EIGHTEENTH CENTURY

tives, especially those written in the latter part
of the Middle Ages, we find the phrase that some
saintly person died in the " odour of sanctity."
Literally, it appears to have been regarded as
meaning a perfume of holiness, but on investigation
it seems to have had its origin in a belief of considerable antiquity.

The Egyptians from early times associated certain odours with their deities.   Thus Isis was believed to have a wonderful odour which she could
transfer to others, and Osiris was said to emit a
perfume which he was able to communicate to
those whom he loved.

The Persians believed that the righteous, after
death, gave forth a sweet odour, and in their texts,
the person approaching the blissful regions was
surrounded by a perfumed breeze.

In one of the tragedies of Euripides, when
dying, Hippolites exclaims: " O Diana, sweet goddess, I know that thou art near me, for I have
recognised thy balmy odour."

The idea that Paradise has a pleasant odour is
found in early Jewish, Gnostic, and Christian writings.   Spiritual persons and martyrs were also
believed to possess this fragrance, and of St. Poly-
carp it was said, that he was so impregnated with

the sweet odour of Christ, that he seemed as if anointed with early perfumes.

In Mallory's History of Prince Arthur, he says that when Sir Launcelot's companions found him dead, they noticed " the sweetest savour about him that they ever smelled."

That curious odours are emitted by sick persons suffering from certain diseases is a well-known fact, and some years ago an American physician called attention to the matter and claimed that the " odour of sanctity " ascribed to certain saints had a neuropathic explanation. He declared, that sometimes the odour may have been due to disease, or emitted during conditions of hysterical excitement or religious exaltation. He instanced that persons who have long suffered from suppurative conditions, emitted an aromatic odour somewhat like strawberries, which was produced by the invasion of the pus by the bacillus pyocyancus, also that in cases where turpentine had been administered, they diffused an odour of violets.

Dr. George Dumas, of Paris, afterwards made a careful investigation of the subject, especially in cases in which mention is made of the " odour of sanctity " in the lives of certain saints, and was able to supply a physical explanation. " The odour," he states, " varies, and has been compared

131

to the perfume of the lily, the rose, the violet, and the pineapple."

In the case of St. Teresa, he believed that the so-called "odour of sanctity" was caused by diabetic acetonæmia, as the breath of diabetics is well known to have a peculiar sweet smell. He concludes, that it is therefore possible that individuals may emit an odour due to certain physiological conditions, as in cases arising from perspiration of the body, and to this the "odour of sanctity" may be attributed.

CHAPTER XIV

FUMIGATION BY AROMATIC SUBSTANCES AND THE HYGIENIC VALUE OF THEIR ODOURS

THE belief that the fumes from burning aromatic substances that have a strong and penetrating odour will purify the air and also the body goes back to very early times. The Babylonians and Assyrians employed them, with certain incantations, to drive away the demons that were supposed to cause disease, about three thousand years ago, and so the idea survived throughout the ages. Even at the present time the popular method adopted to get rid of an offensive smell is to mask it by one that is more powerful, and as a rule, little faith is placed by the public in disinfecting and antiseptic agents that are odourless.

Hippocrates, Criton, and other early Greek physicians classified odours as medicinal agents, and fumigations by aromatics formed part of their treatment of disease.

This belief in the hygienic value and remedial virtues of aromatic gum-resins, sweet-smelling woods and plants, continued throughout the Middle Ages.

Sometimes they were exposed fresh or dried, so that the odours given off were diffused in the air, or they were reduced to powder and burnt, so that the fumes should pervade the atmosphere. During the visitations of the Plague in the Middle Ages, fumigations were largely employed to destroy the supposed " aura " or poison of the disease, which was generally believed to be in the air. A writer on medicine in the seventeenth century recommends for this purpose " such things as exhale very subtle sulphurs, as the spicy drugs and gums." Among these he includes benzoin, storax, frankincense, and all aromatic roots and woods, and " such drugs as are from a vegetable production, and abound in subtle volatile parts, are of service to be exhaled into the air."

One of the chief methods employed in combating the great Plague of London was fumigation with sulphur, saltpetre, and ambergris, which were believed at the time to be the most effective agents in killing the poison of plague wherever it lodged.

In the first great visitation of the pestilence in 1563, every householder in London was ordered to lay out wood for making fires in the streets on three days a week.

134

Pitch and faggots were burnt in the streets by the Lord Mayor's command during the epidemic of 1603, and on the next visitation in the time of Charles I, strong-smelling substances, pitch, charcoal, and incense, were burnt in earthen pans out-of-doors and in the houses.

During the Great Plague, fires were ordered to be lighted in the streets at 8 p.m. and every twelve hours. Six were to be made on each side, and each parish was to provide the fuel and collect the cost, and the watchmen were to keep them burning. Fires made with pine or woods that gave out a pungent smell were thought to be most effective. Gunpowder was flashed in pans, and scraps of leather and horn were burnt, on account of the fumes they gave off.

Saltpetre, tar, and resin were ordered to be burnt on coal fires in rooms which had been infected, in the hope that the fumes would rid the house of the dread visitor.

The Deanery by St. Paul's was fumed twice a week with sulphur, hops, pepper, and frankincense, and all letters that passed through the post-office were fumed over steaming vinegar.

Before the epidemic reached its height, a French quack doctor called Angier came to London, who claimed to have been successful in stopping plague

135

infection at Lyons, Paris, and Toulouse with a fumigation he had invented. It was known as " Angier's Fume " and was soon in great demand. He succeeded in deceiving Lord Arlington, the Secretary of State, and the Privy Council, and the Lord Mayor and Aldermen of London were ordered to give Angier " all encouragement and distribute his medicaments." The celebrated " Fume " was eventually found to consist of sulphur, saltpetre, and amber.

Another fumigation which had considerable popularity was one made by a Dr. Atkinson. It consisted of dried Angelica roots, reduced to powder and steeped in white vinegar for three or four days. When used, the liquid was to be put into a pan, which was then placed on a hot brick, and employed to fumigate the clothing or inhaled with the breath when fasting.

Tobacco also was largely used as a disinfectant and as a preventive of infection, and even children were made to smoke, in the belief that in so doing they would escape the plague. The tradition remained long afterwards, that those who sold and handled tobacco had immunity from plague.

In July 1760 a rumour spread throughout London, causing great consternation, that plague had broken out in St. Thomas's Hospital. It for-

136

tunately proved to be false, but the following morning the demand for the herbs, rue, and wormwood in Covent Garden was so great, that is caused the price to rise 40 per cent. over the normal, and gardeners were employed all the day in bringing supplies of these herbs to the market.

Some years ago attention was called to a statement that cases of tuberculosis were much less common in the flower-growing districts of France than in other parts of the country. This was attributed to the antiseptic effects of the essential oils of the plants in general. It was also noted, that in the laboratories where the oils from the flowers were prepared, the majority of the workers remained remarkably free from diseases of the respiratory organs, which was also said to be due to the air being impregnated with the odours from the various essential oils.

The matter was then carefully investigated by Chamberland of the Institut Pasteur in Paris, and by Cadeac, Meunier, and Smetchensko. The results of their experiments were communicated to the French Biological Society by Charrin, who supported their conclusions. They may be summarized as follows: they found that the micro-organisms of glanders and yellow fever were easily killed by essential oils, the most effective being cinnamon, thyme, French geranium, Indian verbena, lavender, patchouli, angelica, juniper, sandal, and cedar.

In a further test of the action of the oils upon organisms usually encountered in the air, on walls, or in the human body, certain bacteria were exposed to the emanations from essential oils for various periods. The results went to prove that many of the bacteria were killed in less than an hour by the evaporation of certain oils, and in some cases after only a few minutes. Arranged in the order of their bactericidal properties, these essential oils are as follows: Cinnamon, cloves, verbena, lavender, patchouli, angelica, juniper, sandal, cedar, thyme, lemon, pine, wormwood, and extracts of jasmine and tuberose.

These investigations have proved of great importance, and show that in ancient times our progenitors often reached similar conclusions, either by instinct or from practical experience.

An idea has long prevailed that flowers, if left in a sick-room during the night, cause head-ache and generally have ill effects. There may be some truth in the belief, but any such effects do not proceed from their perfume or emanations, but more likely from the carbonic acid they give off in a closed room during the night.

Before leaving the subject, mention should be

138

made of Omeltschenki's experiments on the bactericidal properties of the essential oils of flowers. He found that the bacillus of typhoid fever was killed in 45 minutes in air impregnated with the vapour of oil of cinnamon or valerian, and that the bacillus of tuberculosis was destroyed in twenty-three hours by oil of cinnamon and in twelve hours by oil of lavender or oil of eucalyptus.

CHAPTER XV

ONE of the earliest-known perfumed waters, the use of which has survived for centuries, is Hungary Water. There is a tradition, dating from 1370, that the original recipe for its preparation was given by a hermit to Queen Elizabeth of Hungary, who became so beautiful by its use, that at the age of seventy-two her hand was asked in marriage by the King of Poland.

It is said to have been originally made by distilling the tips and flowers of rosemary with aqua vitæ, which is the first mention of the employment of alcohol for extracting the essential oil from a plant.

The next in point of interest, if not in antiquity, is Lavender Water, which may be said to be one of the oldest English perfumes. The Lavendula vera, the plant from which the essential oil is

140

obtained, is common in many countries in Europe and grows as far north as Norway, and south in Italy, as well as in northern Africa. The earliest mention of lavender known is in the work of the Abbess Hildegard, who lived in the twelfth century, and in which she describes the strong odour and many virtues of the plant in a chapter headed " De Lavendula." In 1387 there is record of cushions being made for Charles VI of France, to be stuffed with " lavende "; and in Wales it is mentioned as a medicine in the manuscript book of the " Physicians of Myddvai " that was written in the latter part of the fourteenth century.

The plant was well known to the writers of the herbals of the sixteenth century, and is recommended for its remedial properties.

It has been cultivated in England from the sixteenth century, especially in the districts of Mitcham, Carshalton, and Beddington in Surrey, also at Market Deeping in Lincolnshire for centuries, and at Hitchin in Hertfordshire since 1568. Owing probably to the special suitability of our climate and soil, the English oil has always been regarded as being greatly superior to that obtained from plants in other countries, and commands the highest price.

The plants flower in July and August, and are then cut with the stalks of full length, tied up in mats, and carried to the distillery, where they are transferred to large stills as gathered. The oil distilled from the flowering heads alone is of a superior quality, and the flowers, even when rubbed between the fingers, give a delightful perfume, which is due to the essential oil they contain. The oil should be allowed to mature for three years before being used.

An oil is distilled from the lavender which grows wild in Piedmont and in the higher districts of the south of France, also near Avignon, but is of poor quality and perfume.

The Lavender Water of the perfumer is really an essence made by diluting the oil with alcohol and sometimes blending it with others.

The earliest recipe we have found for Lavender Water is in a manuscript written about 1615, in which it is directed to distill the flowers with canella, wallflowers, galingall, and grains of paradise, in water.

The product was taken internally to relieve pain, as well as being used as a perfume.

The use of lavender for placing between linen in the housewife's press or cupboard, to perfume

142

the sheets and prevent moth, goes back to the sixteenth century.

One of the last of the old London street cries to survive is that of the seller of lavender, who is still to be heard in July in some of the districts of south London singing:

Come and buy!   Come and buy my sweet lavender!
It is only two bunches a penny.

Thus it was no doubt chanted centuries ago, when London was visited by the plague, for then lavender, as well as other strong-smelling herbs, was in great demand for preventing infection from the dread disease.

Eau de Cologne, like Lavender Water, appears to have been originally employed as a remedial agent when it was introduced early in the eighteenth century, but has survived and still remains in use as a favourite toilet water and perfume.   Its popularity is probably due more to its so-called refreshing properties than the sweetness of its odour.   The former property is chiefly caused by its volatility and the rapid evaporation of the alcohol, as well as to the essential oils of which it is composed.

It is said to have been originated by two brothers,

143

Johann Maria Farina and Johann Baptist Farina, who came from the village of Sante Maria Maggiore near Domo d'Ossola, in Italy, and settled in Cologne, where they started a small business with fancy and silk goods in 1709. In order to increase their trade, Johann Maria commenced to make " Aqua Admirabilis," a cordial water for which there was some demand at the time. This proved so successful that about 1730 they began to send it to other countries. During the Seven Years' War, when many foreign troops were quartered in Cologne, it became increasingly popular for its remedial properties, especially with the French, who carried its reputation back with them to France, where it became known as Eau de Cologne, from the name of the city of its origin.

There is another story that it was first made in Milan by Paul de Feminis, who migrated to Cologne in 1690, and that he passed the secret of his formula on to his nephew, Jean Antoine Farina, in France, who began to make it in Paris in 1806.

In any case, Eau de Cologne appears to have been originated by an Italian, named in France, and made in Germany.

Rennie, who investigated the composition of the

perfume a century ago, concluded it was prepared with spirit of rosemary, eau de mellisse, eau des Carmes and the essences of bergamot, neroli, cedrat, and lemon.

Another early French recipe is given as follows: " Esprit de Vin à trente degrés, dix pintes; Essences de Bergamote quatre onces; de Cédrat, une once; de Citronune once; de Lavante deux gros; de Rosmarin deux gros; de Menthe un gros; de Girofle un gros; de Thymun un gros; de Neroli une once." The ingredients are to be mixed together and well shaken, but not distilled.

Apparently Eau de Cologne did not become universally popular until the early part of the nineteenth century, when its use became widespread and it soon became famous throughout Europe.

Byron alludes to it in his letters, and when Coleridge visited Cologne at the close of the eighteenth century, although he counted " two and seventy stenches, all well defined, and several stinks " in the famous city on the Rhine, he fails to mention Eau de Cologne. Experts say, that it is impossible to make a good Eau de Cologne with English spirit, but latterly this difficulty has been overcome.

The formulæ and processes employed in making the best-known brands are still trade secrets, but

L

the following recipe given by Piesse is interesting and gives excellent results. Take of—

Oil of rosemary . .	1 oz.
Oil of neroli pétale . .	1½ oz.
Oil of neroli bigarade . .	½ oz.
Oil of orange zeste . .	2½ oz.
Oil of citron. . . .	2½ oz.
Oil of bergamot . . .	1 oz.
Spirit (from grapes), 60 per cent.	3 gallons

Mix and shake well together. The citrine attars should first be added to the spirit and the mixture then distilled, the rosemary and neroli oils being added to the distillate.

Among other favourite toilet waters of the eighteenth century was Honey Water, which, according to George Wilson, apothecary to James II, " smoothes the skin, and gives one of the most agreeable scents that can be smelt."

Honey Water contained essence of musk, cloves, coriander, vanilla, benzoin, orange-flower water, alcohol, and water.

Imperial Water also had a great reputation for rendering the mouth sweet and the skin clear. It was prepared by distilling frankincense, benzoin, mastic, gum-arabic, cloves, nutmegs, pine-nut

146

kernels, sweet almonds, and musk with brandy, which no doubt when diluted formed an agreeable and aromatic mouth wash.

Florida Water is of more recent invention and was first made in America, where it is still more popular than in Europe. In odour it resembles a mixture of Lavender Water and Eau de Cologne, with the addition of a little oil of cloves, cassia, and lemon-grass.

The fragrant and aromatic odour of Russia leather is now known to be due to birch-tar oil, distilled from the wood and bark of the Betula alba. The origin of its perfume was long regarded as a secret and a monopoly of the Russian Government.

Referring to a statement that in the Bodleian Library at Oxford there was a book four centuries old still fragrant with Attar of Roses, a writer in the " Bodleian Quarterly Record " states:

" The only scented book is one which came from Monte Cassino, and which, in transit, had been partly saturated with some essential oil. There are, however, distinctive perfumes in various parts of the Library. No one can fail to note the rather earthy smell of the Diocesan Records in the Gough Room, the aromatic scent of the russia-bound books in the Mason Room, and the mellow odour eman-

147

ating from the library of Francis Douce. . . .
The importance of perfume as an essential amenity
of a library was not overlooked by our Founder,
who, when the Library was to be visited by James
I, gave orders that the floor should be rubbed
with rosemary, ' for a stronger scent I should not
like.' "

Snuff-taking, which became so common a habit
in the eighteenth and nineteenth centuries, is in
reality but a method of using perfumed tobacco.
It is stated that two-thirds of the snuff made, owes
its fragrance to ammonia, the tobacco merely serv-
ing as a medium to bring the ammonia to the nose.
The effect thus produced on the olfactory nerves
is combined with the aromatic constituents of the
tobacco.

Of the many varieties of snuff made, such as
Scotch and Rappee, the basis is the ground-stalks
of the tobacco leaf, together in some, with a proportion of the leaf itself.

In the process of manufacture the powder is
moistened with water in which some ammonia has
been dissolved. It is then left to ripen or ferment
for a month or two, to develop a flavour.

Some varieties are then perfumed with attar
of rose and others with essence of bergamot.
Tonquin beans, lavender, vanilla, and cascarilla

148

bark are sometimes employed to give fragrance to tobacco and sweetness to the odour.

In France the perfuming of snuff was carried on to a greater extent in the eighteenth century, and the oils of cedar, neroli, orange-flower, and jasmine, also civet and musk, were often employed for the purpose. The method of using musk was to mix 20 grains in a mortar first with a little sugar, and when they were thoroughly incorporated, to add them to the ground tobacco a little at a time. Ambergris was sometimes used in the same way, and the snuff thus perfumed was called the " Roman Odour."

Cigar makers in Cuba sometimes use aromatic plants to perfume the tobacco leaf before manufacture, and pack the cigars in boxes made from sweet-smelling woods like cedar and the wood of the juniper tree of the Bermudas. The odour of cedar in particular, blends remarkably well with tobacco and improves the flavour, and also the aroma of the smoke. Cigars readily take up the perfume of the box or case in which they are kept, and it is stated that patchouli leaves are able to impart to them the quality of age.

Cedrela wood is now chiefly used for making cigar boxes, which are also sometimes sprayed with perfume.

149

Cigarette tobaccos are also often perfumed before they are passed into the machine, and Virginia, Turkish, and Egyptian are each sprayed with a differently blended odour.

In tobacco prepared for chewing, rum and extract of liquorice are often added to improve the flavour.

DISTILLING LAVENDER

CHAPTER XVI

PERFUMES OF THE EIGHTEENTH AND NINETEENTH
CENTURIES

DURING the eighteenth century, the practice of perfuming not only the clothes but the person, came into vogue with the use of powder-patches and the carrying of the handkerchief in the hand, which were regarded, with the cane, as the necessary adjuncts of the beau monde.

That this fashion was carried to excess and the lure and fascination of perfumes were regarded seriously, is reflected in a Bill that was introduced into Parliament in 1770. It reads as follows:

" That all women, of whatever rank, profession or degree, whether virgins, maids or widows, that shall from and after such Act, impose upon, seduce and betray into matrimony, any of his Majesty's subjects by the scents, paints, cosmetic washes, artificial teeth, false hair, Spanish wool [a wool impregnated with carmine used to colour the skin], iron stays, hoops, high-heeled shoes, and bolstered hips, shall incur the penalty of the law now in force against witchcraft and like misdemeanours, and that the marriage upon conviction shall be null and void."

If this Bill had become law, certainly no one could complain that the bachelors of the time had not been well protected!

It is said that the churches, assembly-rooms, and public halls reeked with the varied odours affected by those who frequented them.

From advertisements in the newspapers of the time the demand for perfumes was considerable and shops for their sale were established. One of these was kept by Charles Lilly in the Strand, previously mentioned, who sold " snuffs and perfumes which refresh the brain in those that have too much for their quiet, and gladden it in those who have too little to know the want of it."

Then there was Mr. Ferene, of the New Exchange, who styled himself " Perfumer to the Queen," and whose " Rare Dentifrice was so much approved at Court." It is interesting to know that it contained " iris roots, pumice stone, cuttel bone, mother-of-pearl, coral, and pounded brick."

Another Strand perfumer was Mr. Perry, whose shop was at the corner of Burleigh Street, who sold " many precious scents used by those of high degree."

A famous London perfumer in the time of

152

THE LABORATORY OF A LONDON PERFUMER IN THE EIGHTEENTH
CENTURY

153

Queen Anne was William Bayley, who opened a perfumer's shop about 1711 in Long Acre, which at that time was considered a fashionable part of town. From thence he removed to Cockspur Street in 1739, where he carried on his business at the sign of " Ye Olde Civet Cat."

In spite of the prevailing fondness for perfumes, Beau Brummell, who was regarded as the arbiter of style and good form of his time, discouraged the using of perfumes, and is said to have remarked that, "no man of fashion should use them, but should send his linen to be washed and dried on Hampstead Heath."

Geographical situation and climate naturally have an important influence on the cultivation of the flowers that yield the choicest perfumes. Although the strong-smelling aromatic gums and other substances come from the warm climes of India, Ceylon, and countries of the Far East, yet Europe produces the roses that yield the finest attar. The south of France, especially the coast of the Mediterranean, the region of sweet-smelling flowers, owes superiority to its natural situation and climate. Cardinal Richelieu is said to have been the first to call attention to the value of the orange-flower groves of Provence, and the cultivation of flowers on the sun-drenched hills of the Var, began

154

to supply the great demand for perfumes which arose in France in the eighteenth century.

Now, as is well known, the country from Grasse to Nice is one great flower garden, and the cultivation of perfume-yielding plants has become an important and wealthy industry. At the foot of the Esterelles grow the sweetest-smelling violets, while the orange trees with their fragrant flowers and also the tuberose flourish and grow there to perfection. From the district around Cannes, roses flourish in great variety, and the tuberose, cassié, jasmine, and orange-neroli are largely cultivated. From Nîmes come rosemary, thyme, and lavender; Nice is famed for its lovely violets; and farther east, along the Italian Riviera, carnations grow luxuriantly. From Italy we get the iris and bergamot; and in the south and in Sicily the lemon and orange trees grow in great profusion.

On the other hand, in colder climes, the finest hyacinths and other odorous bulbous plants come from Holland; while in England, the lavender and peppermint grown in Surrey and Hertfordshire yield the most valuable essential oils of their kind in the world.

Although the perfume of most flowers is secreted during sunshine in the day, there are

155

curious exceptions, and others only yield their scent in the evening or at night. These include the tobacco, Cestrum nocturnum, Lychnis vespertina, Hesperis tristes, and the Nyctanthes arbor tristes, the last-named being only odorous at night. The Habenaria bifolia, which is odourless during the day, begins to give off its perfume about eleven o'clock at night, gradually decreasing in strength towards the dawn and entirely disappearing at sunrise.

A curious circumstance connected with the perfumes emitted by certain flowers, is the development of the odour at the time when some insects are most active. Some plants, like petunias, have only a slight odour during the day, but have quite a strong perfume in the evening, when they are attractive to certain moths. The dark pelargoniums also, which have no odour in the daytime, smell like hyacinths at dusk, and are then visited by night moths. Other flowers which are odorous in the sunshine and attract bees, give off no perfume after sunset. This of course can be explained, and is no doubt due to the warming influence of the sun on the essential oil in the plant.

It has been conjectured that there may be some connexion between the colours of flowers and their odours, and Cohler, in making some experiments

156

on the subject, found that white flowers come first among those giving sweet odours, by a large majority. Yellow flowers are next, and those of a red colour follow closely. Those of blue, violet, and green come far behind, and last of all the flowers of orange or brownish hue.

So far we have only mentioned flowers that emit a sweet-smelling perfume, but there are others that give off repulsive and evil odours which are not so well known. Among these are the mouse mushroom (Tricholoma myomyces), which has an odour like that of mice, a species of orchis smells of goats, and the leaves of the Spiræa ulmaria have an odour similar to carbolic acid. The stinking hellebore, as its name implies, has a most unpleasant odour, and the leaves of the tooth-leaved maiden plum of the West Indies, when bruised, emit a sulphurous smell, and birds that happen to break them are said to fall asphixiated and are unable to fly away for some time afterwards.

The Arum dracunculus, which has a large liver-coloured flower, exhales an offensive odour so like putrefying carrion that blow-flies and other insects mistake the flower for decomposed meat, and come to it from all quarters to deposit their eggs.

There are several other plants which, owing to

their repulsive odours, although their flowers are of considerable beauty, are called carrion plants.

There are also some plants which give off odours that are more curious than actually offensive, such as a fungus or morel of the marchella species, which on being bruised smells like roast beef, and some varieties of crane's bill that have an odour very like roast mutton. The flowers of the yellow water-lily (Nuphar lutea) are sometimes called the " brandy-bottle," on account of the similarity of their odour to that spirit, and the catkins of the goat-willow have the same smell. The horse-shoe vetch (Hippocrepis comosa) has an odour like cheese, and the Philadelphus coronarius has a flavour and a smell similar to cucumbers.

There are instances in which very dissimilar odours are emitted under certain conditions by the same plant. Thus the Tritelia uniflora aspecus, a species of white lily that grows in the neighbourhood of Buenos Ayres, has the perfume of violets, but when the plant is bruised it has an odour like garlic.

The art of the perfumer lies not so much in making the simple odours, which generally consist of the solution of an attar or essential oil extracted from a plant in alcohol, as in the blended perfumes

158

called "bouquets," which contain several ingredients. Among the earliest of these is the essence of Chypre, originally known as Eau de Chypre, which is said to date from the time of the Crusades. The name is believed to be derived from the Isle of Cyprus, of which King Richard I assumed the title of King, and it is probable that the perfumed water was introduced into Western Europe by the knights who came back from the Crusades, who brought with them some of the perfumes from the East. In the sixteenth century it was used in the form of a dry perfume. In the eighteenth century the Essence or Extract of Chypre became a popular perfume in France and has continued a favourite scent. It is said to be a blend of musk, ambergris, vanilla, Tonquin bean, orris, and rose.

Reference has already been made to Frangipani, and the essence under that name has continued in use to the present day.

Another well-known perfume is Rondeletia, which was named by its originators after Gulielmus Rondeletius, the botanist, who wrote a great work on natural history in the sixteenth century. His name is also perpetuated in the Rondeletia odorata, a sweet-smelling flower that grows in the West Indies. The perfume is said to be a blend of the odours of musk, lavender, cloves, and vanilla.

Peau d'Espagne, or Spanish Skin, which consists of soft leather impregnated with ambergris, musk, or civet, was probably first used for making perfumed gloves and was introduced into England from Spain in the sixteenth century. Small pieces of the skin are still employed by those who like its odour, for perfuming note-paper.

Two favourite perfumes used in France in the early nineteenth century perpetuate the names of the ill-fated Marie Antoinette and Marie Joséphine.

Of the older English perfumes, the " Ess. Bouquet " and " Ess. Violletta " appear to be among the first on record. The former was originated by a London perfumer about 1711, and became a favourite scent throughout the Georgian period. It was followed by " Wood Violet," which was introduced as an essence about 1832; and near the same time a perfumed English Lavender became fashionable in Bath. It became a favourite scent for use on the handkerchief and for linen, and this essentially English perfume has remained popular ever since.

Among other scents much used about the

middle of the last century, which may be called old English perfumes, were White Rose, Moss Rose, Jockey Club, Lily of the Valley, Stephanotis, Millefleurs, Verbena, Heliotrope, New-mown Hay, Ylang-ylang, Opoponax, Jasmine, Jonquil, Patchouli, and Peau d'Espagne.

THE CARD OF AN OLD LONDON PERFUMER

CHAPTER XVII

PERFUMES FAVOURED BY ROYAL AND
DISTINGUISHED PERSONAGES

THE special perfumes favoured by royal and other personages present an interesting phase in the power of attraction exercised by certain odours. Generally, when a liking is once acquired for a certain perfume, it is usually constant, and the odour that appeals is generally preferred to any other.

Records have come down to us of the favourite perfumes of some English sovereigns which are not without interest from an historical point of view.

King Edward VI had a special liking for the odour of the rose, and a recipe in a manuscript of the sixteenth century records how it was prepared to perfume his apartments.

It is directed " to take 12 spoonfuls of bright red rose-water, the weight of sixpence in fine powder sugar, and boil it on hot embers and coals softly, and the room will smell as though it were full of roses; but you must burn sweet cypruswood before, to take away the gross air."

Perfume, among other things, appears to have had a special attraction for Henry VIII, and among the Ashmolean manuscripts there is a recipe describing how a favourite one was made for the " King's most Excellent Majestie." It was prepared as follows:

" Take 6 spoonfuls of rose-oil and of rose-water 6 spoonfuls, and a quarter of an ounce of fine sugar. Mix and add 2 grains of musk and 1 ounce of ambergris. Boil together softly for 5 or 6 hours and strain."

This would form a very thick syrupy liquid and would smell powerfully of ambergris, which was probably the odour that he preferred.

Queen Elizabeth's fondness for perfumes has already been mentioned, and she is reputed to have had a very keen sense of smell. Like her Tudor predecessors, she appears to have had a special fondness for the rose. Her special perfume is said to have been made as follows:

" Take 8 grains of musk and put in rose-water 8 spoonfuls, 3 spoonfuls of Damask-water, and a quarter of an ounce of sugar. Boil for five hours and strain it."

There is another recipe for a " dry perfume "

for Queen Elizabeth, that was composed of
" Compound water 8 spoonfuls, the weight of twopence in fine powder of sugar, and boil it on hot
embers softly and half an ounce of sweet marjoram dried in the sun, and the weight of twopence of the powder of benjamin. When dried
this powder is very sweet."

According to existing records, the Emperor
Napoleon had an almost feminine fondness for
perfumes, and a special liking for the odour of
Aloes Wood and Eau de Cologne, which he used
in great quantities. The Aloes Wood cost him
72 francs an ounce, and, according to his perfumer's accounts, he occasionally bought a large
flask of double extract of Spanish Jasmine, but his
consumption of Eau de Cologne was phenomenal.
He always used it when washing, and poured it
over his neck and shoulders in profusion. Madame
de Rémusat states that he used 60 " rouleaux," or
bottles, a month. He also appears to have had
a peculiar fondness for Windsor soap, for which
Chardin, his perfumer, charged him 2 francs a
tablet in the year 1808.

His fondness for Eau de Cologne is evidenced
from his perfumer's quarterly bill in 1806, which
contains the following items:

164

162 bottles of Eau de Cologne .	423	francs
20 superfine sponges. . .	262	,,
26 ornamental pots of Almond Paste (Pâte d'Amande) .	366	,,

In another bill in 1810 there is a charge for 144 bottles of Eau de Cologne at 300 francs, and a large flask of extract of Spanish Jasmine at 40 francs.

A few years later the Emperor apparently found a perfumer who supplied him with a better quality, for there is a bill for " Improved Eau de Cologne " for the Emperor's use dated 1812–13, for supplying 108 cases, each containing 6 rouleaux, at 17 francs per case.

When Napoleon returned from Elba, he transferred his custom to J. Tessier at the " Sign of the Golden Bell " in the Rue Richelieu, who supplied him between March 20th and April 30th with the following items that are entered on a bill:

4 cases of Eau de Cologne . .	24	francs
2 cakes of Orange-flower soap .	6	,,
6 cakes of Windsor soap . .	7.50	,,
3 superfine white sponges . .	30	,,
2 hair-brushes (mahogany) . .	18	,,
2 rheumatism brushes (mahogany)	21	,,

The Empress Joséphine shared her husband's fondness for perfumes, but she had a special liking for strong-smelling essences, and above all for musk. Her dressing-room is said to have been redolent with its odour, to which Napoleon frequently objected.

She is said to have acquired her taste for powerful perfumes from Martinique, and, according to an observer of the time, she was rarely seen without carrying a well-scented lace-bordered handkerchief in her hand, which she constantly held to her nose.

According to a venerable ledger that belonged to one of the oldest Court Perfumers in London, King George IV must have had a great liking for perfumes, and spent a considerable amount on a particular scent he affected.

The story of its first introduction to him has a touch of romantic interest. It happened, it is said, at a State ball, perchance when he was treading a measure or a stately minuet with the beautiful Princess Esterhazy, that a waft of a charming perfume came to him which at once attracted his attention. He made enquiries as to its origin, and the Princess informed him of a particular essence she was using, which afterwards became the favourite perfume of the King.

166

This old ledger of the Court Perfumer of the eighteenth and early nineteenth centuries contains some interesting records and the names of many notable people of that period.

First on its yellow-stained pages is the account for perfume supplied to " the King's most excellent Majesty." In 1821 the bill for perfume amounts to £16 17s. 6d. The following year, however, a much larger quantity was supplied, and there are items of £17 4s. on April 19th, 1822, and again on May 21st, £17 14s., the total amount to the end of December being £263. In 1823 the account reaches £288 9s. 6d., and in 1828 the perfume bill amounts to £500 17s. 11d.

In the year 1803 there is an account for the Duke of York of £143, for " perfume supplied to his Royal Highness." The names of the King and Queen of Hanover appear in 1834, the Empress of Russia in 1834, and that of H.R.H. Princess Charlotte of Wales in 1795, together with many other names of ladies of rank and fashion of the time.

King William IV evidently did not share his royal brother's liking for perfumes, as his account is only about a twentieth part of the sum spent by his predecessor on the throne.

In 1814 the Queen of Wurtemburg's name

167

occurs; and later on, in 1828, that of the Duchess of Kent, the mother of Queen Victoria.

Although one does not usually associate politicians with a love of sweet odours, it is a significant fact that the names of Lord Palmerston, Lord John Russell, and Mr. Canning, according to this old record, are among those who used a considerable quantity of perfume.

The favourite perfume of Queen Victoria is said to have been the English " Ess. Bouquet." Queen Alexandra, from the time of her marriage, when Princess of Wales, is said to have had a preference for Essence of White Rose, a perfume which she used until the time of her lamented death. Her sister, the Czarina of Russia, generally used Essence of Chypre, and the late Queen Olga of Greece was fond of the same perfume.

CHAPTER XVIII

ON THE MAKING OF PERFUMES

THE substances employed in the manufacture of perfumes may be divided into three groups: first, those of vegetable origin; second, the odoriferous substances of animal origin; and third, those produced artificially or by synthetic products, which are now very largely used.

It is rarely that there is a uniform distribution of an essential oil throughout a plant. Sometimes it is to be found in the petals, as instanced in the rose, jasmine, and mimosa, or in the flowers and leaves, as in the violet and lavender. In other plants it is found in the leaves and stems, as in verbena and patchouli; in the bark, as in cinnamon; in the wood, as in aloes and sandal; in the roots, as in angelica, and vertivert; in the fruits, as in lemon, orange, and bergamot; in the seeds, as in bitter almonds; or in the pods, as in vanilla; and in gums or gum-resins, as it is found in myrrh, frankincense, and storax.

The essential oil, or attar as it is often called, when extracted from the flower, is said to be due to excretory products, formed during the metabolism of substances which functioned in the life of the plant. That odours have a relationship to the functions of animals is evidenced in the animal substances like musk and civet, which will be referred to later.

There are several methods employed for separating the odoriferous principles of flowers and plants, the chief being known as maceration, enfleurage, distillation, and expression, to which may be added the use of solvents.

The process known as enfleurage, now so generally employed on the flower-farms in France, is by no means modern, as the Romans used a method for extracting the perfume of roses by steeping the petals in fat when making their unguents.

This operation, which is still considered the best means of obtaining the true, delicate perfume of the flower, is carried out in the following manner.

Panes of glass about 2 feet by 3 feet are set in square frames about 3 inches in depth, and on the glass a layer of fat is poured about $\frac{1}{4}$ inch thick. On this the flower petals or buds are strewn and allowed to remain for from 10 to 72 hours. The frames are then laid one over the other, and

170

the flowers are changed so long as the plants continue to bloom.

For essential oils of the same plants, coarse cotton cloths are saturated with the finest olive oil and laid on a frame of wire gauze, instead of glass, and on these the flowers are laid, and allowed to remain until fresh blooms are ready. After this process has been repeated several times, the cloths are subjected to great pressure to remove the perfumed oil.

The essential oil, or attar, when dissolved, or in solution with alcohol, is called an essence, extrait, or esprits.

The blended perfumes, consisting of several oils dissolved in alcohol, like the well-known Jockey Club, are known as " bouquets," and vary according to the proportion and variety of the attars employed.

In giving a brief description of some of the chief substances employed in perfumery, the first place in importance must be given to the rose, the " queen of flowers," which excels not only in beauty but in yielding the most exquisite perfume known to man.

The rose has a literature of its own, and more legends and traditions cluster round it than any other flower. It has been esteemed for its perfume from the earliest times, and at no period more than in the early Christian era.

It was associated by the ancients with Venus, goddess of Love, and the expression " sub rosa " is said to be due to Cupid having bribed Harpocrates, the god of Secrecy, with the dedication of his mother's flower, the rose, in order that he might preserve a discreet and invariable silence concerning the love-affairs of the beautiful goddess.

The ancient Greeks, when desirous of paying a compliment to their most flowery orators, would say " they spoke roses."

If on Creation's morn the King of Heaven
To shrubs and flowers a sovereign queen had given,
O beauteous Rose, he had anointed thee,
Of shrubs and flowers the Sovereign Queen to be.
(Hymn to Sappho.)

In Persia from the earliest times the flower has been almost reverenced, and the national poetry is full of allusions to the lovely flower. Their poet Hafez sings:

When the young rose in crimson gay,
Expands her beauties to the day,
And foliage fresh her leafless boughs o'erspread

In homage to her sov'reign power,
Bright regent of each subject flower;
Low at her feet the violet bends its head.

The Persians filled their houses with the fragrant
blooms, and " beds of roses " in their apartments
were literally true.

According to Ibn Khaldun, about A.D. 810 the
province of Farsistan was compelled to provide an
annual tribute of 30,000 bottles of rose-water to
the treasury of Bagdad. There is also evidence
that an essence was made in Persia about 1612.

In England it became a national flower from
the time of the Wars of the Roses, and will never
cease to be an emblem of the country throughout
the British Empire.

Time was when the rose-girl's cry was heard
in our London streets, but now, with many other
quaint customs, it is only a memory. Probably
few remember the lines:

Come, buy my sweet roses, ye fair ladies all,
And bless my poor mother and I;
Nor fresher, nor sweeter boasts basket or stall,
Come, buy my sweet roses, come buy.

The perfume of the rose is due to its attar or
essential oil, which is obtained by distilling the
flower with water.

173

Beyond the story of its discovery by Noorjeehan Begum in Cashmere, the first allusion to it occurs in the Persian work mentioned of 1612.

The region which produces the finest plants for the purpose of perfumery is Turkey and Bulgaria. At Adrianople large farms for cultivating and growing the Rosa damascena cover extensive tracts of the country and extend over 14,000 acres. This rose bears semi-double light red flowers of moderate size.

Broussa and Uslaak, Eastern Roumelia, and also the country south of Philippopolis are famous for their roses. In India, Ghazepore is also a centre of a rose-growing industry.

The season for gathering roses in Eastern Europe is from the latter part of April until early June, when from sunrise the plains of Bulgaria look like a vast garden full of life and fragrance. Hundreds of children are to be seen gathering the flowers into baskets and sacks, the air being impregnated with a delicious perfume and the scene enlivened by singing, dancing, and music.

The process of distilling the oil is carried out on the farms, often with very primitive apparatus, in a shed. A copper still, consisting of a cistern with a still-head and a condenser, or cooling tube, which passes through a wooden tub filled with

174

water, together with a large flask used as a receiver, comprise the apparatus. The still is placed on a furnace made of bricks or stones, a hole being provided with a tube to carry off the smoke, and wood is used for fuel. The receiving flasks when filled with the rose-water are allowed to cool. The distillate is then again distilled a second time, and received in flasks of peculiar shape which act as separators. The attar, being lighter than water, rises to the top, and is then collected as an oily layer and placed in small tin drums for transport.

Roses are also cultivated in France, at Grasse and Cannes, the perfume being extracted by enfleurage, the result being the pomade à la rose.

In the latter part of the last century the Cabbage Rose (Rosa centifolia) was cultivated near London for the purpose of making rose-water, but the industry has now died out.

An attempt is now being made by experts to restore the old perfumes to new rose species, and some good results have been obtained.

Almonds have been known from a very early period and are mentioned in the Babylonian tablets about 1500 years B.C., also in the Book of Genesis, when Israel commanded his sons to carry with them into Egypt a present, consisting of the products of Palestine, among which were almonds.

175

Bitter almonds are also mentioned by Scribonius Largus in the first century. Sweet almonds were used in enormous quantities in mediæval cookery, and the oil extracted from them has always been highly valued.

The essential oil of almonds employed in perfumery is derived from the distillation of the leaves of any of the laurel tribes, from the kernels of stone fruit, and the outer skin of the bitter almond. It does not exist ready in the nut, but is produced from two bodies, amygdalin and emulsin, it contains, after water has been added. Its poisonous properties, due to hydrocyanic acid, are well known. The artificial product prepared from benzol, and known as Essence of Mirbane or nitrobenzol, which was the first of the synthetic perfumes to be discovered, has now almost superseded it.

Balm, the attar or oil distilled from the Melissa officinalis, has been employed from an early period for its odour, especially in France, in the southern parts of which it grows wild.

It was believed to possess invigorating properties when taken internally, and formed one of the ingredients in the celebrated Eau des Carmes, so largely used as a cordial in the seventeenth century. It is said that Charles V, when in the

176

Monastery of St. Yuste, used it daily in his bath and inhaled it on a handkerchief to refresh and preserve his intellect.

Basil, which is regarded as the most sacred plant of India, is the Tulsi or Holy Basil dedicated to Krishna, and named after Tulasi, beloved of Krishna, the Hindu Daphne. It is grown in many native houses, where it is daily watered and worshipped by the household.

" In the Deccan villages," says Birdwood, " the fair Brahminee mother may be seen early every morning, after having first ground the corn for the day's bread and performed her simple toilet, walking with glad steps and waving hands round and round the pot of Holy Basil planted on the four-horned altar built up before each house, invoking the blessings of the gods on her husband and children."

Benzoin, a gum-resin obtained by exudation from the Styrax benzoin, a tree that grows chiefly in Sumatra and Java, is now mainly used in making incense. It does not appear to be mentioned before the fourteenth century, and in mediæval times was known as benjamin, and frequently entered into the composition of the dry perfumes then in use. A tincture or solution in spirit was formerly employed in blending per-

N

fumes, and it is still used in making face-washes
and applications for the skin. It forms the chief
ingredient in the well-known preparation called
" Friar's Balsam."

Bergamot is an essential oil expressed from the
fruit of the Citrus bergamia, a small tree re-
sembling in flowers the bitter orange, which is
cultivated at Reggio in Calabria. It does not
appear to have been used until the seventeenth
century, and is mentioned in " Le Parfumeur
François " in 1693. It is said to form the chief
ingredient in the perfume Ess. Bouquet.

Cascarilla, the bark of the Croton eluteria, a
small tree that grows exclusively in the Bahamas,
need only be mentioned for the aromatic perfume
it gives off when burned. It formed one of the
ingredients in the Frangipani incense, and is still
employed to give an aroma to the smoke of
cigarettes.

Cassié, Acacia farnesiana, like mimosa, is one
of the acacia species and is largely grown in the
district round Cannes and other parts of the
Riviera. The perfume is obtained by macerating the flower-heads in purified fat, from which
a pomade is made; or an oil is prepared by employing olive or almond oil in place of the solid
fat as a medium for maceration. It is a favourite

178

odour, largely used in perfumery, and enters into the composition of many well-known bouquets.

Calamus, Acorus calamus, is the aromatic sweet-flag that grows on the margins of streams and lakes throughout Europe, in the Far East, and in North America. The root has been used in India from very early times, and was known to the Greeks centuries before the Christian era. It has a pleasing odour due to an essential oil which is distilled from it. When powdered, it was a common ingredient of the dry perfumes formerly used.

Carnations, of which there are many species, are cultivated largely on the French and Italian Rivieras. The white, pink, yellow, and red are grown near Grasse for their perfume, which is extracted in France in the form of pomade. In Holland, where carnations are also cultivated in some districts for the purpose of perfumery, solvents are employed for extraction.

Olibanum, or frankincense, is the gum-resin obtained from several species of Boswellia that grow in the hot and arid regions of East Africa, the south coast of Arabia, the Somali country, and also in India. Notwithstanding long and careful investigation, the olibanum trees are still imperfectly known. It has been used from a period of

179

remote antiquity, and has always been highly valued for its aromatic perfume, for which purpose it formed one of the most important ingredients in the incense of the Jews.

Olibanum was one of the most important aromatics with which the Phœnicians and Egyptians carried on trade with the Arabs in ancient times. The fragrant gum-resin is obtained from the leaves and barks of the trees, and even exudes as a milky juice from the flowers. The method of collecting in the Somali country is by making a deep incision in the tree and peeling off a narrow strip of bark below it. This is left for a month, when a fresh incision is made, but deeper. After the third month, the incision is again repeated, when the gum is ready for collecting and the large clear globules are scraped off into a basket, the inferior quality which has run off down the tree being packed separately. The gum, which is called Lubân by the Arabs, when first collected is very soft, but it soon hardens. In the hot season the aroma given off by the gum perfumes the air and, it is said, can be detected from a considerable distance. In colour it varies from a pale yellow to brown, which sometimes has a greenish hue, and it contains a small amount of essential oil.

Geranium oil is obtained from the Pelargonium

180

capitatum, or rose-leaf geranium, the leaves of
which when distilled give a rose-like odour something approaching attar of rose, but coarser and
stronger. It is cultivated both in France and
Turkey, and has often been used to adulterate the
true attar, as a hundredweight of the leaves of the
plant, which often grows to a height of from 3 to
4 feet, will yield 2 ounces of essential oil.

Heliotrope, the delicate perfume of which is so
popular, is obtained from the Heliotropium peru-
vianum by maceration or enfleurage from the
flowers.

Ylang-ylang, or " the Flower of Flowers," is
obtained from the Canaga odorata, a plant indigenous to the Philippine Islands, where it is cultivated chiefly near Manilla. The flowers, when
distilled, yield an attar which has a delightfully
delicate odour, and is used in perfumery diluted
with alcohol, alone, or blended with other essential oils. It was first sent to Europe in 1864.

Jasmine, a favourite perfume in the Far East,
is cultivated in the south of France, Tunis, and
Algeria. The flowers of the Jasminum odoratissi-
mum yield their beautiful perfume when distilled
with water. This process is repeated, using the same
distillate over fresh flowers, until an essence is
obtained. The perfume is also obtained by en-

fleurage, the resulting pomade being dissolved in alcohol.

Lilac flowers yield their perfume to certain fats, and by the process of enfleurage an essence is obtained, but this natural odour has now been largely superseded by that made synthetically.

Mignonette, or réséda, which has such a charming and delicate odour, and is a favourite in our flower gardens, does not yield a perfect essence. An Extrait de Réséda is made in France by dissolving the pomade prepared from the flowers in alcohol, but it lacks the peculiar sweetness of the fresh plant.

Myrrh, which is more correctly classed as an aromatic than a perfume, is a gum-resin obtained from the myrrh tree, Balsamodendron myrrha, and other species, that grow in Arabia and on the Abyssinian coast of the Red Sea. Like Olibanum, it is one of the earliest aromatics known, and has been employed throughout the ages as an ingredient in incense, unguents, and perfumes. It exudes from the trees in the form of a milky juice, which becomes a reddish brown as it hardens. It yields a small amount of essential oil, as well as gum and resin, and has been much esteemed as a drug from ancient times. It is still used in medicine, and forms an ingredient in several preparations of the

182

British Pharmacopœia. Myrrh trees abound on the hills near Shugra, east of Aden, and the gum from them is collected by Somalis, who cross from the opposite coast for the purpose and pay a tribute for the privilege to the Arabs.

Neroli, or Orange-flower Oil, is largely employed in perfumery, and is prepared from the fresh flowers of the bigarade, or bitter orange, by distillation with water. The water which is distilled in the process, after the removal of the oil from the surface, forms the Orange-flower Water so much used for toilet purposes. It is described by Porta in the sixteenth century, who refers to its " most exquisite fragrance." The name " Neroli " is said to have been given to it on account of its use by Anne-Marie de la Tremoille-Noirmoutier, second wife of Flavio Orsini, Duke of Bracciano, and Prince of Nerola or Neroli, who employed it for perfuming her gloves, which were called in Italy " Guanti di Neroli." Two distinct odours are produced from the flower, according to the method employed for extraction. One is by distillation with water as already mentioned, and the other by macerating the flowers in a fat which forms the orange-flower pomatum. This, when digested in alcohol, forms the extract of orange-flowers that is so largely used as a perfume.

183

The oil of Petit Grain, which resembles Neroli, is obtained by distillation of the leaves and shoots of the bitter orange or of the Portugal or sweet orange. This is also employed in making perfumes, and especially in the manufacture of Eau de Cologne.

The orange is among the most valuable of perfume-giving trees, for from the flowers two distinct odours are obtained, the peel of the fruit yields another, and from the leaves and shoots a further perfume is derived.

Opoponax is a gum-resin which is said to be obtained from the bisabol tree, that grows in Somaliland. It is thought by some to be the myrrh of the Bible. An essence of the perfume is prepared by macerating the gum in alcohol.

Orris, or iris, is the root derived from several species of the plant which grows throughout Europe, Macedonia, and Asia Minor. The Iris germanica and the Iris pallida are cultivated for the production of the root in the neighbourhood of Florence. It was largely used on account of its violet-like odour by the ancient Greeks and Romans, and Elis and Corinth were famous for their unguents of orris. Pliny states " the best comes from Illyricum and the next from Macedonia," and that it is used as a perfume and a

184

medicine. It is believed that the Iris germanica is the Illyrian iris of the ancients, and that it was probably not introduced into Italy before the early Middle Ages.

The arms of Florence, a white lily or iris on a red shield, is thought to point to the fact that the city was famous for its connexion with the plant. Petrus de Crescentiis of Bologna, who lived in the thirteenth century, mentions the white as well as the purple iris, and states when the root should be collected.

Orris root and anise were used in England in the time of Edward IV to perfume linen, and are mentioned in the wardrobe accounts in 1480. All the species of the plant were cultivated in England before the end of the sixteenth century.

The root, when distilled with water, yields a crystalline substance called Orris camphor, which has a beautiful odour and is found floating on the distillate. Besides its use in perfumery, powdered orris root is extensively employed in making dentifrices and sachet powders.

Patchouli is obtained from the leaves of the Pogostemon patchouli, a plant which grows in Bengal, Java, Ceylon, and the Malay coast. It owes its powerful and peculiar odour, the strongest that is derived from the vegetable kingdom, to an attar,

185

which is separated by distilling the leaves and stems. From this an extract is made by dissolving it in alcohol.

It has long been known in the Far East, but does not appear to have been used in Europe until about 1826, and its importation is said to have been due to the French manufacturers of imitation Indian shawls. The genuine shawls, which are valuable, were always distinguished by their peculiar odour, and that was the only thing which the makers of the imitation articles could not produce, until eventually the secret was discovered that the perfume was due to patchouli. They then began to import the plant in order to give the same odour to their shawls as those made in India.

Patchouli leaves, dried and powdered, are often used as an ingredient in sachet powders and pot-pourri.

Sweet-pea, Lathyrus odoratus, is much appreciated for its charming and delicate odour. It is extracted from the flowers by enfleurage with an odourless fat, and the pomade thus made is dissolved in alcohol to form an essence.

Rhodium oil, formerly extracted from Convol-vulus scoparius, is now chiefly made by mixing the oils of cedar-wood, sandal-wood, palm rosa, and geranium. It was used for blending with other

186

oils. The odour has a curious attraction for dogs and other animals, and they will often follow the trail for considerable distances.

Rosemary, one of the old English herbs of fragrance and often cultivated in our physic gardens, grows also in many parts of Southern Europe, generally near the sea. Pliny attributes to it many properties, and its virtues were much esteemed in the Middle Ages, which may be judged from the fact that it was chosen as one of the plants which Charlemagne ordered to be grown on the Imperial farms. It is mentioned in an Anglo-Saxon Herbal in the eleventh century, and was probably cultivated in England before the Norman conquest. The essential oil was distilled by Raymond Lully about 1330, and was generally believed to have preservative properties. Its peculiar odour is due to an attar which is obtained by distilling the whole plant with water, the production of which is chiefly carried on in the south of France. It is still often employed as an ingredient in hair-lotions, as it is believed to promote the growth of the hair, and also enters into the composition of Eau de Cologne and Hungary Water.

Rue, another aromatic herb, has been used from times of antiquity, and is mentioned in the Gospel of St. Luke in connexion with " tithes of mint and rue and all manner of herbs." It has long been reputed to possess prophylactic properties and was much in demand during the great epidemics in the Middle Ages.

The custom of placing sprigs of rue in the Central Criminal Court at the Old Bailey on the first day of the Assizes, took its rise in the belief that the Judge and others would be thus protected from the infection of gaol fever, from which the unfortunate prisoners who had been confined in old Newgate so frequently suffered.

Sandal-wood has been esteemed for its odour and fragrance from a very early period, especially in the Far East. It is mentioned in the Nirukta, or writings of Yaska, one of the oldest Vedic works known, that dates from about the fifth century before the Christian era. Its odour, which is due to an essential oil, is extracted by distillation, and was employed as early as the ninth century in Ceylon for embalming the bodies of the Princes.

The wood is obtained from a small tree, Santalum album, that grows chiefly in the mountainous parts of the Indian peninsula, especially in Mysore and in the Madras Presidency. It is also found in the islands of Timur and Sumba of the Eastern Archipelago. In the religious ceremonies of the Brahmins, Hindus, and Chinese it is extensively used in the incense offered to the deities in their temples.

The Hindus also use large quantities in celebrating their sepulchral rites, and the wealthier class show their respect for a deceased relative by adding sticks of sandal-wood to the funeral pile, while the powdered wood, made into a paste with water, is employed for making the caste mark. The odour is said to be disliked by the white ants, and so the wood is largely used for making cases and coffers for storing clothes. In perfumery the oil is chiefly employed for blending with other odours.

Spikenard, so highly valued for its odour and fragrance in ancient times, is now generally believed to have been derived from the Nardostachys jatamansi, a plant belonging to the Valerian order, which grows chiefly in the mountains of Bhutan and Nepaul. It was probably brought by traders into Palestine and farther west in the form of an unguent, at a period prior to the Christian era. It was greatly esteemed by Eastern nations, and considered very valuable in Western countries and was only used on special occasions, hence the allusion in the New Testament to the " alabaster box of ointment of spikenard, very precious." It was probably used for softening and perfuming the skin, after washing, by people of wealth.

189

Storax, or styrax, has been known from a remote period, the name having been applied to two substances of different origin, one being a resinous body and the other called liquid storax. Both were known and used by the Greeks and Romans, but the former is now identified as the aromatic resin, famous for its fragrant odour from the first century down to recent times.

It is obtained by exudation from the stem of a small tree, the Styrax officinalis, that grows in Greece and Asia Minor. It has a peculiar odour, and is mainly employed by perfumers to give permanence to a scent, for, like benzoin, it has the property of fixing a perfume and making it last longer.

Tonquin beans are the seeds of the Dipterax odorata, that grows in the forests of British Guiana, and have a characteristic and powerful odour due to an oil and a crystalline body called coumarin. The latter has also been found in several plants, including the melitot and sweet woodruffe.

An essence or extract of the bean is made with alcohol, which is used in blending several perfumes, or when reduced to powder it forms a favourite ingredient in sachet powders.

Tuberose, Polianthes tuberosa, so largely cul-

190

tivated in the south of France, yields a charming and favourite odour which is extracted from the flowers by enfleurage. The pomade so formed is digested with alcohol, and after being allowed to stand for about a month, is decanted off and forms the essence so frequently employed by the perfumer. The perfume of the tuberose is especially more fragrant after sunset, so the process of enfleurage is usually carried on in the dark. On account of its rapid volatility, a little storax is usually added to it to give it permanence.

Verbena, a plant with many traditions and mysterious superstitions mainly connected with witchcraft, yields an attar with a strong and pungent odour which is often used by the perfumer. It is specially cultivated for this purpose in Valencia, where it grows luxuriantly, and the oil is extracted from the leaves by distillation with water.

The violet, Viola odorata, with its sweet and delicate odour, probably comes next to the rose as a favourite among perfumes. It is cultivated extensively in the south of France, especially in the neighbourhood of Nice, also in Italy in the country around Florence, for its use in perfumery.

Its odour is due to an attar which is extracted by enfleurage or by maceration. From this, an essence is made with alcohol which is of a fine green

191

colour and retains the natural odour of the flower.

Vitivert, or cus-cus, is extracted from the Vertiveria zizaniodes, a large grass that grows abundantly in Southern India and Bengal, where it has been used since the twelfth century. Its odour is due to an attar which is employed by perfumers for blending, and many favourite bouquets are said to owe their fascination to this essential oil. In India it is placed in drawers to perfume linen and prevent the ravages of moths, or it is made into screens for windows and doorways, which when moistened with water diffuse a delightfully cool odour.

Vanilla beans, employed both for their perfume and for flavouring, are the fruit of a climbing orchid of various species, among which are the Vanilla planifolia of Mexico and Vanilla pompona of the West Indies. When first gathered they have no smell, the odour being produced by a fermentation which goes on during the process of curing, usually carried out by boiling or exposure to the sun.

CHAPTER XIX

ODOURS DERIVED FROM ANIMAL SECRETIONS

THE odours of animal origin play a very important part in the composition of perfumes. Some of them have been used from a very early period, and for centuries their sources of origin were enveloped in great mystery and were associated with many strange legends.

Musk was known and used in India, China, and Persia for centuries before it was brought to Europe, whence it probably came through Arabia. It is mentioned in the list of presents sent to the Emperor of Rome by Saladin in 1189. Curious stories are related of its origin, and for a long time its true source was unknown.

Pomet, in his " History of Drugs," written in the seventeenth century, says: " It comes from the Musk Cat. There are a great many of these animals in the Kingdoms of Tonquin and Boutan, and in divers Parts of Asia. That which we call musk, is a corrupted blood which is collected under the belly of this animal after the manner of an impostume, and when it is ripe, the Beast by In-

o

stinct, goes to rub itself against a Tree to break it; and this corrupted blood being dried in the Sun, acquires a strong smell that is very disagreeable, which it ought to retain when it is pure, and has not come into the hands of the Jews in Holland and other places, who sophisticate it with Earth, dried Blood and other Contrivances."

Tavernier, about the same period, states: " The best Sort and great quantity of Musk comes from the kingdom of Boutan, from whence they carry it to Patna, a city of Bengal, to traffic with the people of that country. All the musk that is sold in Persia comes from thence."

On account of its high value and the many hands it passes through, musk has been subject to adulteration for centuries. Tavernier, writing in the seventeenth century, says: " The King of Boutan fearing least these tricks which are play'd with the musk should spoil the trade for it, since it can be had from Tonquin and Cochin China, has some time since, commanded that none of the bladders should be sow'd but all brought open to Boutan which is his place of residence, there to be inspected and sealed with his seal. But notwithstanding all the King's precautions, the People have a cunning way to open them, and put in their small bits of lead which the merchants endure patiently, because

194

it does not spoil the musk but only deceives them in the weight."

The first allusion to it in English literature appears to be in a manuscript written in 1398, in which there is mention of " boxes made to kepe in muske and other spicery." Lanfranc, about 1400, refers to its use in medicine, and Hakluyt in his " Voyages," 1570, remarks: " The Negroes answered againe they had civet, muske and grains."

Musk is a reddish-brown substance secreted in a gland or sac by the male musk-deer, a small animal about the size of a goat, which is found in high altitudes of the Himalayas, and in the great mountain-ranges in Northern India, which extend into Thibet and China. The gland in which the musk is secreted is shaped like a little bag about the size of half a walnut, and is found about the navel of the animal. These are cut off by the hunter, and are called in commerce " musk pods." When the contents are removed from the bag or sac, it is known as " grain musk."

A single pod may contain as much as from two to three drachms of musk, but the quantity varies with the season and depends on the age of the animal. The pods are wrapped singly in paper, and packed in a small rectangular box covered with silk. This box is known as a caddy, and contains a " catty," or about 21⅔ ozs. of musk pods.

Most of the musk used in Europe comes from Thibet, and the Tonquin musk from the Chinese province of Szechuen. Yunan musk is also of Chinese origin, while the varieties called Nepaul and Assam come through Calcutta. Still another kind, known as Cabardine musk, is sent from Northern Chinese ports to Japan.

The musk-deer is hunted by the natives and is either snared or shot. In some of the hill-states in India it was considered as Royal property, and the Rajah kept trained hunters to go after the deer, which are very difficult to track, as they are rarely found at less than 7,000 or 8,000 feet up in the mountains and generally near the line of perpetual snow. The fatigue entailed in reaching these altitudes is very great, and the hunting is attended with many hardships and risks.

The interior of the Himalayas, from whence the chief supply is obtained, is towards Ladâk, Thibet, and Chinese Tartary. As the mountain-ranges extend over many thousands of miles, it is probable that the varieties of musk known as China, Nepaul, and Russian come from near or the same regions.

The Tartar tribes wander from place to place, bartering with the natives of the several countries

HUNTING THE MUSK DEER
(From an old Chinese print.)

who have access to the hunting districts, and so it is frequently found that the musk is often very art-fully adulterated with earth, dried blood, or refuse.

Of the chief kinds of musk in commerce, the Tonquin or Chinese is generally considered the best, the Assam is very strong in odour but is some-what rank in smell, while the Russian is usually poor in fragrance. As a perfume, it is remarkable for its strength and for imparting its odour to any-thing that is brought near it, in so much that at one time the East India Company would not allow it to be shipped in the same vessel with tea.

It has long been used in medicine as a stimu-lant and anti-spasmodic, and was for some time an official remedy included in the British Phar-macopœia. It is still highly esteemed in Eastern countries for its medicinal properties.

For the purpose of perfumery, an essence is made by macerating musk in alcohol for a month, to extract the odour, and this may then be diluted and used for blending with other perfumes.

Powerful though the odour of musk is, curiously enough it is completely destroyed when brought into contact with camphor or bitter almonds.

Musk owes its perfume to a colourless oil, which it yields by distillation and has been named muskone.

198

The origin and source of ambergris, which is probably the most lasting perfume known, was a matter of conjecture for centuries.

Pomet describes it " as the dearest and most valuable commodity in France." He continues: " It is brought to us from Lisbon and is nothing else but a mass of honeycombs that fall from the rocks into the sea. These honeycombs being in the sea, whether by a property of the sea water or by the Virtue of the Sunbeams, are rendered liquid and floating upon the water, as is to be met withal sometimes. M. de Monconys affirms, that he was informed in England that ambergris was nothing but Honeycombs that bees make upon the large Rocks which are on the Sea Side in the Indies which heated by the Sun loosen and fall into the Sea."

Tavernier, in 1646, says: " A Zelander of Midelburg who was Governour of the Isle of St. Maurice found on the Shoar a piece of ambergris of 42 pounds weight."

It was also declared to be a vegetable product allied to amber, which it was originally called, the present name meaning " grey amber."

This peculiar wax-like substance of a marbled ashy colour, which is found floating in tropical seas, is now known to be a morbid secretion found

199

in the intestines of the sperm-whale, and is a variety of intestinal calculus. A recent theory as to the production of ambergris is, that the concretion is due to the hard beaks of octopi swallowed by the whale, which it is unable to digest. This hard matter is the predisposing cause of the secretion, which results in the formation of the substance which the whale eventually ejects, and is found floating in the sea. It is usually found floating in the sea near the islands of Sumatra, Madagascar, and near the coasts of America, Brazil, China, and Japan.

The natural source of the substance and the peculiar conditions under which it is found no doubt gave rise to many of the fabulous stories concerning its origin.

It is mentioned in Howard's " Household Books " in 1481–1490 as " Imber-gres," also by Elyot in his " Castell of Helth " for its medicinal virtues. Ben Jonson thus alludes to it in " Neptune's Triumph ":

Why do you smell of amber-grise
Of which was formed Neptunes' niece.

Ambergris is soluble in alcohol, and the essence thus made is chiefly employed for blending with other perfumes as a fixative and to give them a

lasting property. As a solid perfume it will retain
its odour for centuries, and there is an authenti-
cated record that it has been detected after a period
of three hundred years. It clings to woven fabrics
even after they have been washed and dried, and
the longer it remains the sweeter the odour becomes.

There is one room at Hampton Court Palace
in which a perfume is said to have lingered for over
a century and its fragrance is still perceptible.

Civet, another of the substances of animal origin
employed in perfumery, has been known in Europe
since the early part of the sixteenth century. Like
musk, its origin was at first wrapped in mystery, and
an early writer describes it as being " a thick liquid
found in a pouch which is under the tail of a beast
like a Spanish cat, but much more fierce and
voracious."

Bulleyn, in 1564, alludes to " Muske and Zenet
in every place did abounde "; and Topsell, in his
book on " Fourfooted Beasts " in 1607, mentions a
" Zibeth or Sivet brought out of Africa."

Pomet, who endeavoured to find out the history
of most of the drugs in use at his time, procured
a civet-cat which he kept alive for a year to study
its habits. He states: " It was brought from China
by a person in the retinue of the Ambassadors of

Siam, who gave it to one of my friends, who made a present of it to me in the year 1688. Having kept this creature some days, I perceived, that the wall and bars that enclosed it, were covered with an unctuous moisture, thick and very brown, of a very strong and disagreeable smell; so that all the time I kept this animal, I took care to gather the civet out of the pouch every other day; not without some trouble and hazard, because it put the creature to some pain or apprehension about it; and having done so for some months, I had about the quantity of an ounce and a half. The colour of the drug did not please those I showed it to, though it was well scented, and as good at least as that which is brought from Holland."

The Dutch at this period were evidently the chief distributors of civet, and it is recorded that many of the merchants in Amsterdam kept civet-cats in long wooden cages and had the secretion scraped from them two or three times a week with a wooden spatula. The Dutch civet was said to be light in colour, on account of their practice of feeding the animals on milk and the white of eggs. "This commodity," continues Pomet, "is as difficult to be known as musk. It is for this reason the Hollanders put little printed certificates upon

202

THE MUSK DEER AND CIVET CAT
(From an engraving of the seventeenth century.)

their pots of civet to give it the credit of being pure."

Lemery, the French chemist of the seventeenth century, says:

" The beast from whence it is taken is called in Latin, Hyæna, Catus Zibethicus, in English, Civet-Cat. Merchants buy the young ones and breed them tame, so that a cat that is large and gentle may come to be valued at between four and eight pounds sterling.

" The best civet is made in England, but great quantity is sent from Holland. The West Indian, Barbadian and African civets are next in goodness, but the blackest is the worst that comes from the East Indies. It is much to be preferred to musk because the scent is finer. It comforts the spirits and is good against all diseases of the head and brain."

The Civet in use at the present day is obtained from several animals of the Civet genus, especially the African civet-cat. It is a yellow or brownish unctuous substance which is obtained from sacs or glands in the anal pouch of the animal, unpleasant in appearance and with a disagreeable smell, but the essence prepared from it, when well diluted, has a pleasing aroma. It is used by per-
204

fumers for blending, who say it would be difficult
to imitate some flowers without it.

The essence was often used by men of fashion in
the eighteenth and early nineteenth centuries, and
the practice is alluded to by Cowper in the following lines:

I cannot talk with civet in the room,
A fine puss gentleman that's all perfume;
The sight's enough, no need to smell a beau
Who thrusts his nose into a raree show.

Castor, another animal secretion used in perfumery, is chiefly employed as a fixative. It consists of the dried membranous follicles of the
beaver. They are filled with a strong-smelling
secretion which, when diluted, is not disagreeable,
the odour being due to an essential oil it contains.

Some perfumes have the peculiar property of
increasing the power of others and making them
smell stronger. Thus ambergris, on the addition
of musk, develops a much more powerful odour,
and lavender is similarly affected.

The odours of animal origin are especially valuable to perfumers on account of their fixative
power, as in order to make a perfume lasting,
an ingredient with these properties is necessary.
Musk, civet, ambergris, olibanum, storax and benzoin are chiefly used as fixators in blending.

205

CHAPTER XX

A CENTURY ago no one would have dreamt that the perfume of flowers would ever be derived from the refuse of gas-works and other malodorous materials, and that one day their manufacture would develop into an industry of great importance. Yet, owing to the wonderful advances made in the science of chemistry, the delicate odours of the most sweet-smelling flowers are now made artificially, by the union of certain elements which closely resemble, if they do not equal, the perfumes elaborated by Nature.

Although the processes by which the natural odours are formed in plants is still a mystery, the chemist, in finding out the composition of natural perfumes and their chemical constitution, has accomplished by known methods and made possible their manufacture by the combination of these elements.

The romantic story of this discovery begins about 1834, when Mitscherlich discovered nitro-benzene, but it was left to Collas in 1855 to iden-

206

tify it as the first synthetic perfume, which is now known as essence of mirbane.

The discovery by Cahour that the odour of natural oil of wintergreen was chiefly due to methyl salicylate, led to a process being found to make the oil artificially, and in a similar way from the preparation of benzaldehyde from benzyl chloride in 1868, a method was discovered of making the artificial oil of bitter almonds. In the same year Sir William Perkin, the famous dis-coverer of aniline mauve, produced coumarin, the perfume of hay and woodruff. This was followed by the discovery of vanillin, the odour of vanilla, by Tiemann and Haarmann in 1875, and more important still, ionone, the artificial perfume of violets, which was first made by Tiemann and Krüger in 1898.

Many of these synthetic products have very different odours in accordance with their dilution, and when strong are by no means attractive; some have no smell when in the solid state, and others have disagreeable odours when dissolved.

To put the matter of their discovery in simple language, it was found that the attars of certain plants consisted of certain elements, and the chemist discovered that by varying these he was able to produce different odours.

207

Durvelle divides the chief synthetic perfumes into two classes, viz. those that contain bodies derived from hydrocarbons, phenols, etc., of coal tar, and the others that are prepared from substances derived from essential oils of vegetable origin.

The former are obtained by chemical processes which reproduce the odours of a given constituent of plants, like Heliotropin, the perfume of heliotrope; while others are obtained by mixing various bodies and those that constitute a new perfume, or imitate to some extent natural perfumes.

Among the most important of the odorous constituents of essential oils are bodies called " esters." An ester is a combination of an alcohol and acid, this being brought about by the elimination of water, thus Bergamot, Geranium, and Lavender Oils all owe their perfumes largely to esters.

From coal tar we get Vanillin, Coumarin, artificial Musks, Benzoic Aldehyde, Benzyl Acetate, and Anisic Aldehyde, and practically all of these are now being made in England and France.

Without going into a technical description of these bodies and the methods of their production, mention should be made of some of the principal benzenoid compounds, such as the aldehydes, oxy-aldehydes, phenols, and phenol ethers, that are employed as perfumes.

Among these is citral, which is extracted from lemon-grass oil and has the odour of lemons. It was found that by condensing this body with acetone and treating the product with sulphuric acid, the odour of violets was produced which is known by the name of ionone.

Heliotropin or Piperonal, an aldehyde, has the delicate odour of the heliotrope flower, and is now largely employed in making the cheaper varieties of scents and for perfuming soaps.

Benzaldehyde has a powerful odour of almonds, and is used in blending; while anisic aldehyde, which has the sweet smell of hawthorn, is also much used for perfuming soaps, face creams, and powders.

Amyl salicylate, known as orchidée or tréfol, is used as the basis of many artificial perfumes, and especially those having the scent of clover.

Methyl anthranilate occurs in the natural essential oil of neroli, and is used in the preparation of artificial bergamot, neroli, and jasmine, while cinnamyl alcohol has the sweet odour of hyacinths and is also frequently employed in perfumery.

Alcohol phenyl ethyl has the perfume of the rose and Carvacrol that of marjoram.

P

Besides the odour of lemon-grass, citral also yields the scent of verbena. From geraniol is obtained the perfume of the rose-geranium, and terpineol gives the varied odours of lilac and lily of the valley. It is prepared from oil of turpentine.

Linalol has the smell of aloes-wood, and santalol gives a perfume akin to sandal-wood.

Mignonette, cyclamen, honeysuckle, and ylang-ylang are also imitated, and iso-eugenol has a strong odour of the carnation.

Linalyl acetate when mixed with geranyl acetate gives the perfume of lavender.

Bromostyrolene is used as a basis for such perfumes as hyacinth, jonquil, and narcissus.

Methyl benzoate, known as Oil of Niobe, has the odour of tuberose and ylang-ylang; and benzylidene acetone, prepared by mixing acetone and benzaldehyde, is employed as a basis for the sweet-pea perfumes.

Even the odour of musk is artificially prepared, the process being discovered by Baur in 1888, and is a derivative of s-trinitro-benzene.

The acids and alcohols of the hydrocarbons differ again chemically from the benzaloid odours; thus pelargonic acid is closely connected with the rose perfumes and valerianic acid with the scent of the plants of that species.

Many of the artificially prepared products are placed on the market under various fanciful names, and the processes by which they are made are kept secret.

The chemist, in thus carrying out his processes in making perfumes artificially, is but employing the same substances as are formed in the plants. In spite of this wonderful achievement, however, the results do not and probably never will equal those produced in Nature's own laboratory.

There is a subtle difference between the synthetic and the natural product, and the latter has an aroma and superiority that science with all its marvels has not yet been able to equal.

CHAPTER XXI

THE PHYSIOLOGY AND PSYCHOLOGY OF ODOURS

IT is a well-known fact that the sense of smell varies considerably in individuals and is much more acute in some than in others. This depends on the sensitiveness of the olfactory nerves, the human organ of smell, which are situated at the upper part of the nasal cavities.

They were first recognized by Theophilus Protospameaus, a Greek monk, in the eighth century. The organ is essentially formed by the filaments of the olfactory nerves, which are distributed in minute arrangement in a limited portion of the mucous membrane of the nose. The sense of smell is therefore derived exclusively through those parts of the nasal cavities in which these nerves are distributed. If the nasal cavities be filled with rose-water, no smell is perceived. It is a curious fact that some persons whose sense of smell is quite normal cannot distinguish certain odours. When a perfume is placed under the nose, there is no sensation of smell so long as the breath is held, or breathing is carried on through the mouth.

212

It is common knowledge that there is an intimate relation between the senses of taste and smell, and the same substance which excites the sensation of smell in the olfactory nerves may cause peculiar sensation through the nerves of taste, and may produce an irritating effect on the nerves of touch, but the sensation of odour is yet separate from them.

Man uses the sense of smell in combination with taste much more during mastication and deglutition than during the act of putting food into his mouth, the chief importance of smell in association with taste being to perceive the quality of foods, to influence their selection, and to excite appetite.

Although the susceptibility of man to odours is more extended, he is inferior to animals of both classes in the sense of smell. The distance at which a dog can track his master is extraordinary, and birds of prey will scent a battlefield for a great distance. Pliny affirms, that crows have so acute a sense of approaching corruption that they can perceive certain smells of decay before actual dissolution. Most insects and fishes, also crabs and lobsters, have a keen sense of smell.

Animals, however, do not all equally perceive the same odours, and those perceived by a herbivorous animal are different from those by a car-

213

nivorous one. The carnivora have the power of detecting most accurately by smell the special peculiarities of animal matters, and of tracking other animals by scent, but they appear to have no sensibility to the odour of plants and flowers. On the other hand, herbivorous animals have a very sensitive sensibility to plants and flowers.

The sense of smell is more highly developed among savage races than in civilized man, as instanced in the Indians of Peru, who are able to follow up the scent of game like hunting dogs.

But the sense of smell may be trained to a great extent; thus pharmacists are able to recognize drugs by their smells and physicians can tell certain eruptive diseases by their odour.

Some Ethiopic races and North American Indians are able to track their enemies owing to their remarkably acute sense of smell, which is probably largely due to their mode of living. Hunting and war being their chief pursuits, their physical faculties are thus developed by constant practice.

It has been asserted that every individual has his own peculiar odour which is unperceived by himself.

Berthelot states, that the odour of newly turned soil is due to a minute trace of a camphorated body which is so odorous that even a trillionth part of a milligramme gives a perceptible smell. Odours are remarkable for fixing themselves on the memory, and places and events can often be recalled after many years have elapsed by a smell associated with them.

" Scents are surer than sounds or sights to make your heart-strings crack," wrote Rudyard Kipling, and no one can doubt their power to recall memories of the past.

It is well known by experience how some odours will bring to mind certain towns one has visited, and so recall incidents that happened there.

What true Londoner does not welcome the smell that salutes his nostrils after a prolonged stay abroad—that curious odour, a blend of petrol, tar, and smoke, peculiar to our streets, that may be called the smell of London?

The story has recently been recorded of a certain planter who lived in the up-country in India, that when the manufacturing season was on, he would go into the engine-room for a smell of hot oil, which reminded him of the ship that brought him out from England and which he hoped one day would take him back. This smell of hot oil was a link between him and home. To another individual the odour of burning wood from a newly lighted fire will recall a much disliked schoolroom in which he passed unpleasant hours when a youth, forty years ago. The smell of tar will sometimes recall a certain ship or a sea-port, and many other instances might be mentioned where an odour or perfume will bring back the memory of persons, places, or events that happened long ago.

Many odours that give pleasure to some people are intolerable to others, and the effect of these odours is very marked. Some will even provoke nausea and headache in sensitive persons, while in others they have the power of exhilarating, and if very powerful have an almost intoxicating effect. This extends to the entire nervous system, as instanced in the effect of burnt feathers on a fainting person, and the relief and stimulation afforded to another by the application of aromatic odours such as lavender and rosemary. Certain strong-smelling substances like musk and rose are often disagreeable and even sickly when in a concentrated state, but are pleasant and delightful when diluted.

In Rome, some people find that they are unable to stand the strong odour of certain flowers in that climate, and are unable to sit in a room with them without experiencing highly oppressive sensations which at times produce fainting attacks.

The sense of smell is easily fatigued by long-continued exposure to odours, and those who work regularly in sewers and drains after a time fail to perceive them.

The sensation produced by an unpleasant odour may be succeeded by a stronger smell, but the weaker is still there.

Odours are individual, and no smell appears to have a clear relation to another. It is stated that " while an odour may have the most vivid associations in the mind with other circumstances, the human brain has been unable to abstract odours so that they can be associated one with another." Therefore there is no scale of smells.

Repugnant smells influence us instinctively, and accordingly we reject food that has an evil odour. When subject to an offensive odour, the effect is to make us impatient and irritable; while, on the other hand, if we are in a pleasantly perfumed atmosphere, the tone of the mind alters and we become bright and cheery.

The question is often asked, how is odour conveyed? This may be explained if we realize that the material causes of odours are substances suspended in a state of extremely fine division in the atmosphere or gaseous exhalations, often of so subtle a nature that they can be detected by no other reagent than the sense of smell. Thus vola-

217

tile bodies, disturbing the conditions of the nerves by a chemical action, exert the greatest influence upon the organ of smell.

Some authorities state that the oxygen in the air plays an important part in the diffusion of perfume, as perfume essences can be deprived of odour by excluding oxygen and volatilizing them. This can be recovered instantly when they are brought again in contact with the air.

Substances possessing a very low degree of volatility are those with the strongest odours, as for instance patchouli, opoponax, and cloves; while those which have a high degree of volatility, like rose, calamus, neroli, and bergamot, are weaker and more delicate in scent.

Having then considered what may be called the physiological aspect of the sense of smell, let us try to ascertain how certain perfumes can excite the emotions to a degree which influences the physical and moral propensities.

It is believed by some that the olfactory nerve is so intimately connected with the brain that it is really not a nerve, but part of the brain itself. They cite the fact that an odour will affect the brain almost instantaneously, and that the inhaling of certain vapours will often cause death. That of course must depend whether the vapour is

218

innocuous or not, but the effect of odours on the emotions is a much more subtle matter.

In what, then, lies the lure or attraction which certain odours and perfumes have exerted on people from early times? The French physician Féré attributes it, to some extent, to the genetic functions, with which, he says, the sense of odour has very varied relations.

A great many animals are provided with glands whose special secretions produce at the time of rut a very intense odour, the specific action of which is clear. The odours of these products of animal secretion are not without effect on man.

Musk, especially, plays in many individuals very efficiently the rôle of a genetic excitant, while some perfumes of vegetable origin have a similar effect, among which patchouli and other strong-smelling essential oils may be taken as examples.

Mantegazza records the statement of a lady who declared, " I feel so much pleasure in smelling a flower, that it appears to me I commit a sin."

In certain individuals the lure of the odour becomes very predominant.

" The sweet perfume of a toilet-shop," says Rousseau, " is not so feeble a decoy as one thinks, and I do not know whether to felicitate or condole with the man, wise but sensible, whom the odours of the flowers which his mistress wears at her bosom could not make palpitate."

The most active perfumes are those which come nearest to the odours of the sexual secretions, or which derive therefrom, like musk and civet, which are the basis of many popular perfumes. It is well known that the dog will at once recognize the smell of his master, showing that different people exhale different odours through their cutaneous secretions. The odour of these secretions must vary greatly according to the individual. People with red hair are said to exhale a very distinctive odour. It is said of Alexander, that " he was loved by women more than any other prince, because his sweat was more odoriferous."

Sometimes certain colours exercise a similar lure to odours. Féré records the case of a Parisian for whom women with red hair had an uncontrollable fascination. In the street or elsewhere, if he met a woman with red hair, he would try to come near her, be she plain, beautiful, young, or old, and he would follow her for miles. He states that this impulse was produced on the man even when the red-haired person was at a considerable distance.

The same curious fascination in connexion with some odours is found in animals. The attraction

220

of the smell of valerian for cats is well known, and the odour of the stinking goose-foot (Chenopodium olidum), which is somewhat like putrid salt-fish, and cat-mint (Nepeta cataria) also exercises an extraordinary fascination over the feline animal. The lure of the latter plant is so strong that cats delight to roll in it, and having broken it down with convulsive capers, will tear it to pieces with their teeth.

Dogs are also attracted by the stinking goose-foot and will roll on the plant, but the oil of rhodium has a still more powerful fascination for them, and they have been known to follow the odour for considerable distances.

At one time it was often employed by street-thieves to lure pet dogs. The method used was to sprinkle a little of the oil on the bottom of the legs of their trousers to attract their victims, who would follow the scent; then, when a suitable opportunity occurred, the thief would snatch up the little animal and hide him under his coat.

It has been asserted that women use perfumes to arouse the attractive instinct. Whether this be true or not, there seems to be no doubt that certain perfumes do act upon the emotions, and they have had a lure for the feminine sex from time immemorial.

221

A strange instance of the fascination of a perfume was recorded in a French scientific journal a short time ago, concerning a young woman who developed an intense love for the odour of patchouli. She saturated her linen, clothing, and even the furniture of her apartments with this perfume. Loss of appetite, depression, and insomnia soon followed, and in the end she became a victim to neurasthenia.

There is a curious difference between the odours preferred by women and men. Women, as a rule, show a distinct liking for perfumes in which mint, citronella, rose, violet, and the softer odours are combined; while men have a preference for musk, lavender, cedar, sandal, or perfumes in which they take part. Among Eastern races, however, the more delicate odours are not appreciated, and a fondness for the more powerful and heavy perfumes is pronounced.

Sir William Temple, in his " Essay on Health and Long Life," makes an interesting statement regarding the stimulating effect of odours from his personal experience. He says:

" How reviving as well as pleasing some scents of herbs and flowers are is obvious to all; and what great virtues they may have in diseases, especially

222

of the head, is known to few, but may easily be conjectured by any thinking man.

"I remember that when walking in a long gallery of the Indian House at Amsterdam, where vast quantities of mace, cloves, and nutmegs were kept in great open chests, I found something so reviving by the perfumed air that I took notice of it to the company with me, which was a great deal, and they were all sensible of the same effect."

SIGNBOARD OF A LONDON PERFUMER IN 1739

223

CHAPTER XXII

THE ANTIQUITY OF COSMETICS—ODOURS USED BY PRIMITIVE RACES

MUCH has been written on the use and abuse of cosmetics, and it is not our intention to deal with the subject here, beyond their connexion with perfumes and to show the antiquity of the practice. The idea of beautifying the person and attempting to improve on the natural physical attractions, appears to have been innate in human beings from the earliest times, just as it is found among barbaric races to-day.

There are many causes for this desire common to human beings, to endeavour to make themselves more attractive and pleasing to the eye than their fellows, and among them vanity, rivalry, and ambition are probably the chief forces.

Ideas of beauty have varied among different races throughout the ages, but, judging from the earliest records, the facial features, such as the eyes, the mouth, the skin, and the hair, have been the parts chosen for artificial adornment.

The women of ancient Egypt over three thousand years ago employed paints and cosmetics for this purpose, and their toilets were often quite as elaborate as those of the fashionable women of to-day. To soften their skin they applied perfumed oils and unguents, and coloured their lips and tinted the cheeks with a finely levigated red ochre. Kohl,

THE TOILET OF AN EGYPTIAN PRINCESS
(From a bas-relief of the IVth dynasty.)

a black powder prepared from antimony, was applied with an ivory or wooden bodkin to line the eyes to make them appear larger and more brilliant, and also to darken the eyebrows. Nor were the hands neglected, for the fingers and nails were carefully coloured and stained with henna. Numerous toilet instruments of various forms and

Q

shapes have been discovered, which were probably used for manicuring the nails.

The hair was very carefully tended, and at some periods was worn long, and at others short, in a fashion similar to that of to-day, but elaborately crimped or curled. Before being dressed, perfumed oil was poured over it and it was then combed. Egyptian combs were generally made of bone or wood, with fine teeth on one side and coarse on the other, and were sometimes beautifully carved and ornamented.

The Babylonian and Assyrian women applied stibium, a black powder like the Egyptian kohl, to the lids and corners of their eyes, and rubbed the skin with finely powdered pumice-stone to make it smooth, and applied a preparation of white lead to the face. Great attention was paid to the toilet, and especially to the dressing of the hair, which was worn in long ringlets flowing over the shoulders, confined by a band round the head above the forehead.

The Hebrews adopted many of their habits and customs from the Egyptians, and there are several allusions to the use of cosmetics in the Old Testament. Jezebel endeavoured to add to her personal charms by painting her face, and the prophet Ezekiel mentions the custom of painting the eyes

226

and the decking of the person with ornaments. Henna was probably used for colouring the skin and the Egyptian kohl for the eyes. According to Josephus, the pages who preceded Solomon on ceremonial occasions had their hair profusely pow-

ROMAN LADY USING A COSMETIC

dered with gold-dust, which glittered in the sun's rays with a most brilliant effect.

The toilet practices of the women of early Greece and Rome have been fully dealt with in previous pages. They employed preparations of white lead for the face, and coloured their cheeks and lips with vermilion and pœderos, a root con-

227

taining a red colouring matter like alkanet, which imparts its colour to oils.

The toilet of the Roman woman of fashion was quite an elaborate ceremonial, as thus described by Juvenal:

She hurries all her handmaids to the task;
Her head alone will twenty dressers task;
Psecas, the chief, with neck and shoulders bare,
Trembling, considers every sacred hair.

Face-powders were composed of corn or pea-flour and barley-meal. Crumb of bread soaked in milk, or narcissus bulbs and honey, were sometimes spread on linen and kept over the face at night. A depilatory was used to remove superfluous hair, and a red colouring matter called fucus for the cheeks. Calcined pumice-stone was used as a dentifrice to whiten the teeth, and barley-flour made into an ointment with butter was applied to take away pimples from the face.

Hair dyes were also used by those who wished to change the colour of their locks, but with what success it is difficult to say. A recipe for making a dye to turn the hair black is stated to have been prepared from leeches, which had to be left to decompose for sixty days in an earthen vessel with wine and vinegar.

228

The hair of the Romans being generally dark, there was a great desire by some to change it to blonde or golden colour, but they knew not peroxide of hydrogen, so much in demand in our time, and for this purpose are said to have employed a kind of soap made from goat's fat and ashes. Martial calls it " Mattiac balls," because they were made in a German city called Mattium. That these applications often did more harm than good, as many do to-day, is evidenced by Ovid's allusion to the lady who destroyed her flowing locks by means of dyes.

Did I not tell you to leave off dyeing your hair?
Now you have no hair left to dye.

When they were unsuccessful in changing the hair to the much-desired golden tint, it was an easy matter to cut it off and wear a wig. Martial thus refers to—

The golden hair that Galla wears
Is hers; who would have thought it!
She swears 'tis hers, and true she swears,
For I know where she bought it.

So, through the ages, one might go on describing the various methods and preparations employed which were supposed by the users to enhance their beauty and add to their attractions. The recipes

229

for cosmetics that have come down to us from the sixteenth century would fill volumes, and no useful purpose would be served by recapitulating them.

Matthiolus mentions in his " Commentary," printed in Venice in 1558, the interesting fact that belladonna was called by the Venetians " Herba Bella donna," on account of a water distilled from the plant being used by the Italian ladies as a cosmetic. They found, on applying it to the eyes, it dilated the pupil and made them appear larger and more brilliant. It was employed in France in the eighteenth century for the same purpose, and continued in use until recent times; but since it was found to affect the sight, the danger of its application was realized.

In the time of Louis XV the craze for cosmetics, face-washes, and powders was universal among the ladies of the Court. The skin was often plastered with pastes until little of the natural complexion was visible, and immense sums were spent by the fashionable beauties in these preparations of the toilet. It is said that etiquette prescribed the use of a particular kind of perfume every day, which caused Versailles to be named " la Cour parfumée," and the beauty-doctors of the time reaped a rich harvest.

230

During the period of the Empire the use of cosmetics began to wane, but the love for perfumes so common to the French continued, and still remains.

The cult of beauty is practised by women to-day. and the desire to make themselves attractive by artificial aids is as strong as it ever was. Probably at no time has the powder-puff and lip-stick been in so much evidence in public as at present. Of their use and abuse the dermatologists are the best judges, and could doubtless say a great deal.

The makers of such preparations at the present time, however, have the advantage over their predecessors in being able to utilize the wonderful advances made in the science of chemistry in recent years. The materials are freer from impurities and the basis of most of the modern face-powders consists of wheat- or rice-starch, orris-root powder, with zinc oxide or bismuth oxide, together with French chalk or talc in varying proportions, to which perfume is added.

A favourite application for the skin in the last century was " Pomade Divine," which was believed to have many virtues. It was composed of cloves, nutmegs, benzoin, orris root, storax, cinnamon, camphor, and lard, perfumed with Attar of Rose. The ingredients were placed in a pan altogether

231

and allowed to stand in a water-bath for five hours, and then strained.

The basis of the lip-sticks now so generally used chiefly consists of paraffin or white wax, with carmine as the colouring matter. Mineral colouring agents should never be employed. The black powder called Kohl used at the present day is said to be made from the soot collected after burning gum benzoin, incense, and almonds.

Powder and patches were closely associated in the seventeenth and eighteenth centuries, and although the use of the latter has almost entirely disappeared, what little is known of their history may be of interest. The name of their originator is lost to posterity, but there is a tradition that the little black patch was first used by a Court beauty to cover a disfiguring mole on her cheek, and she found the effect so satisfactory she continued to wear it.

The fashion spread rapidly, as it was considered to give an additional charm to the face, and, in contrast with powder, gave a peculiar attraction to the features.

Patches were cut from small pieces of " court plaster," a simple adhesive, spread on black silk, which derives its name from having been first made for the ladies of the Court.

232

They are first mentioned by Bulmer in 1650, who gives an illustration, in "The Artificial Changeling," of a lady's face elaborately decorated with patches of various shapes and sizes, among which is a miniature coach-and-four.

Evelyn remarks that "painting and similar tricks of the toilet did not become established among *respectable* women before the spring of 1654."

The popularity of the fashion and the excess to which it was carried may be judged from the fact, that a bill was introduced into the House of Commons on June 7th, 1650, by the Puritan party, for the suppression of "the vice of painting, wearing black patches and immodest dress of women," but after being read a first time, it suffered the fate of other measures of the kind and was dropped.

The fashion, after declining for a time, was revived in the reign of Queen Anne and continued during the eighteenth century. In an old number of the "Spectator" there is an account of an amusing scene which took place at a theatre, where two opposite boxes were filled with ladies all carefully patched. In one party the patches were all worn on the right cheek, and in the other on the left. The former represented the Whigs and the other the Tories.

233

Thus they sat glaring at one another, each one of the political dames doing her best in defiance to stare the other out.

Patches were shaped in varied form, as small circles, stars, crescents, and many other devices, and carried in small boxes of gold, silver, or tortoiseshell and ivory, often having a small mirror in the lid.

Depilatories for removing superfluous hair have been used for over a century, and those now employed for this purpose generally consist of alkaline sulphides, such as calcium, sodium, or barium, mixed with powdered quicklime and diluted with starch or talc. A favourite preparation of this kind used in Eastern harems is called " Rushma," and is said to be composed of arsenic sulphide, lime, and sulphur.

The employment of perfumes and applications to the skin is common to civilized and uncivilized races alike, and natives of barbaric countries are imbued with the same idea of making themselves attractive by artificial aids.

The negroes of Africa have a great fondness for strong perfumes, and apparently enjoy odours which are repugnant to civilized man. The employment of coco-nut and palm oils to coat the skin has probably been used by instinct from time

234

immemorial as a protection from the burning rays of the sun, and a pride is taken in giving the body a shining and glossy appearance. The oil is sometimes perfumed with aromatic herbs or woods, and certain tribes employ a native unguent which is by no means agreeable to Western tastes.

Hutchinson mentions a preparation made and used by the natives in the district of Fernando Po called " Tola pomatum," and says: " The first thing of which one is sensible when approaching a village is the odour of ' Tola pomatum,' wafted by whatever little breeze may be able to find its way through the dense bushes." A woman before marriage covers her body with this preparation, " until she looks like an exhumed mummy, with the exception of her face, which is smeared with a white paste said to be symbolic of purity. Later on, her whole body is similarly coated, and this forms her bridal attire."

In some parts of Nubia an oil perfumed with aromatic roots is rubbed into the skin to give elasticity to the limbs, and the perfumes affected by the Arabs are generally those in which musk predominates.

Livingstone says that the Griquas take the greatest pride in " smearing themselves with grease and red ochre, whilst the head is anointed with a

235

blue pomatum made of mica. The particles of shining mica falling on the body are thought to be highly ornamental and the mixture of colours very attractive."

It was formerly customary in Egypt to place a grain of ambergris in the coffee-pot, to add to its aroma and flavour. The perfumes now preferred are musk and civet, and olibanum is sometimes chewed to perfume the breath. In the houses of the rich the guests were sprinkled with rose or orange-flower water, and sweet-smelling woods and gums were burnt in the apartments. The perfuming vessel, called Mibkhar'ah, used for burning the perfume, consisting of aloes-wood, benzoin, or cascarilla, was handed by the servant to his master, who would waft the smoke towards the face and beard with his right hand.

In the Philippine Islands the native women use an unguent prepared with coco-nut oil perfumed with the flowers of the *alangilan* or *san-paquita*, and the Javanese employ a yellow cosmetic to enhance the brilliancy of their bronze-tinted complexions.

The Polynesian races pride themselves on the various methods and colours they employ in painting the face and other parts of the body.

In the Marquesas Islands a highly perfumed

236

coco-nut oil is used for the body, and the juice of the *papa*, a native product, has a reputation for preserving the skin and making it smooth.

The women of Tahiti pay great attention to their teeth and hair, and daily anoint the latter with a preparation called *Monoi*, which is composed of coco-nut oil perfumed with sandal-wood, or a native root called *Toromeo*. They are fond of placing sweet-smelling flowers in their hair, especially the delicately scented *tiare*, which is similar to jasmine.

The Indian races of South America have a great love for perfumes, and Wallace mentions a native scent they prepare which has a beautiful odour and is highly esteemed on the Rio Negro. It is known as *Umari*, and is extracted from a native tree, the Humirium floribundum, by raising portions of the bark and inserting under it pieces of wool, so as to absorb the perfume, which is expressed from them at the end of a month.

In the methods of painting the face the North American Indians are renowned, and it is said they will spend unlimited time in thus adorning themselves with their wonderful designs in varied colours.

Such instances might be multiplied indefinitely, but sufficient have been mentioned to show that in

237

all parts of the world this fondness for odours that give pleasures to the senses and the cult of physical attraction has existed throughout the ages.

By whatever motives it is inspired, this desire to add to the charms that Nature has endowed the person appears to be innate and common to mankind.

INDEX

Abeer, 40
Active perfumes, 320
Ægyptium, 17
Alabaster box of "ointment of spikenard," 45
  containers, 18
  perfume bottles, 68
Alchemists and perfumes, 92
Alcohol phenyl ethyl, 209
Alexander the Great, 26
  perfumes for his palace, 26
Almonds, 175
Ambergris, 199
  origin of, 199
American Indian's adornment, 237
Amyl salicylate, 209
Anacreon, 76
Andaman Islanders, 51
"Angier's Fume," 136
Animals and sense of smell, 213
Antiochus Epiphanes, 26
  his love for sweet odours, 26
Antiphanes, 72
Antiseptic properties of essential oils, 137
Apollonius on perfumes, 66
Apothecaries, 89, 91
Arabia Felix, 28
  grandeur of its cities, 30
Arabs and chemistry, 30
  flowers prized by the, 36
  fondness for musk, 32
  narcissus valued by the, 36
  passion for roses, 33
  preserve their rose blooms, 33
  their love for perfume, 28
Arms of Florence, 185
Aromatic gums, early use of, 7
  perfumes used in past ages, 11
  ribbon, 58
  waters, 91

Aromatics for the plague, 134
Artificial perfumes, 206, 211
Arum dracunculus, 157
Aspalathos, 63
Assam musk, 198
Assur-banipal, 25
  use of cosmetics, 25
Assyrian, care of the hair, 25
  paint for the face, 26
  use of stibium, 26
  women, 25
Assyrians, fondness for perfumes, 24
  incense used by the, 23, 50
  knowledge of fragrant gums, 24
Astyages, King of the Medes, 28
Athenæus, 69, 72
Athens, perfumers' shops, 69
"Atkinson's Fume," 136
Avicenna, 30

Babylon, great market for gums and spices, 25
Babylonia, caravan routes, 11
  trade in gums, 11
Babylonian plain called Eden, 6
  women and their toilet, 226
Babylonians, fumigations employed by the, 23
Baccaris, 72
Bactericidal properties of perfumes, 138
Balm, 176
Balm of Gilead, 44
  cultivated, 4
"Balsam Innocenziano," 96
Banquets, perfumes used at, 14
Bartering a necklace for perfume, 15

Basil, 177
Baths of ancient Rome, 79
Bayley of " Ye Olde Civet Cat,"
    154
Bdellium, 5
Beau Brummell on perfumes, 154
" Beautiful for ever," 128
Bel, golden statue of, 24
Belladonna for the eyes, 230
Benzaldehyde, 209
Benzoin, 39, 177
Bergamot, 178
Binding the head with garlands,
    71
Bitter almonds, artificial oil of,
    207
Boundary stone of land in Eden,
    6
Bouquets, 159
Boutan, 194
" Bridal attire " of a native, 235
Bridal presents, 41
Bromostyrolene, 210
Bucklersbury stalls, 90
Bulgarian rose-fields, 174

Cabbage rose, 175
Cagliostro, 106
Calamus, 8, 179
Calcite vase found in Tutankh-
    amen's tomb, 19
    contents described, 19
Camphire, 45
Canning, 168
Carnations, 179
Cascarilla, 178
Cassié, 178
Cassolettes, 117
Casting bottles, 126
Castor, 205
Catherine de' Medici, 100
Catullus, 86
Cedar coffers for clothes, 111
    wood to perfume cigars, 149
Cedrela-wood cigar boxes, 149
Cestrum nocturnum, 156
Chamberland's investigations, 137
Chaplets and wreaths, 14
Charlemagne, incense used in
    tomb of, 57
Chiksa, 40

Chinese and musk, 41
    musk, 198
    perfumes, 41
Church of England and use of
    incense, 57
Chypre, 116, 159
Cigar perfumes, 149
Cinchona Elixir, 96
" Cinnamon from Krinippos," 65
Citral, 209
Civet, 201
    cat, 201
    for gloves, 120
Cleopatra and her love of per-
    fumes, 15
    Shakespeare's allusion to, 16
    spices to anoint her hands, 16
Coal tar, perfumes derived from,
    208
Coco-nut oil for the skin, 234
Colour for the face, 85
" Concerning odours," 62
Coriander, 8
Cosmetics during the Empire, 231
    in time of Louis XV, 230
    use in ancient times, 224
    used in Egypt, 225
Cosmo Ruggiero, 100
Costly Roman perfumes, 82
Coumarin, discovery of, 207
Court perfumers, 166
Crane's bill, 158
Criton introduces perfumes, 60
Cult of beauty to-day, 231
    of Siva, incense offered in, 54
Curious odours of plants, 158
Cus-cus, 192
" Cushions of perfumed roses,"
    119
Cyprinum, 18
Cyprus, 159
Czarina of Russia, 168

" Damask Perfume," 119
" Damask Powder," 115
Daphne, games held at, 26
Decoration of Thermæ, 80
Depilatories, 234
Děr-el-Bahari, Temple of, 10, 22
Diana of Poitiers, 105
Diorite vases, 18
Dog thieves, method of, 221

Dominicans and perfumes, 96
Doves distribute perfume, 73
Du Barry, 106
Duchess of Braganza's perfume,
  117
Duchess of Kent, 168
Duchess of Parma's perfume,
  117, 118
Duel with patches, 233
Duke of York, 167
Dutch civet, 202

Easterlings of Soper's Lane, 88
Eau de Carmes, 176
Eau de Chypre, 159
Eau de Cologne, 143
  a French recipe, 145
  Byron's allusion to, 145
  story of its origin, 144
Edfu, recipes for making perfumes, 12
Edward VI's perfume, 162
Effect of odours, 217
Egyptian apothecaries, 21
  combs, 226
  customs, 236
  customs, perfumes preferred,
  236
  knowledge of aromatic gums,
  12
  oil of lily, 17
  perfumes, 17, 18
" Egyptian Perfume," the, 64
Egyptian women:
  antimony used by, 22
  henna juice used by, 22
  rouge used by, 22
Egyptians bathe in perfumed
  water, 13
  large consumption of perfumed
  unguents by, 13
Eleusinian Mysteries, incense
  used during, 53
Embalming, 21
  in England in Tudor times, 91
Empedocles of Agrimentum
  stops plague epidemic, 51
Empress Joséphine's fondness
  for musk, 166
Enfleurage, 170
English civet, 204

English Lavender, 155
  water, 160
English perfumes in sixteenth
  century, 114
Eridu, 6
" Ess. Bouquet," 160
" Ess. Violetta," 160
Essence of Civet, 205
  of Cypirus, 66
  of Quince, 69
  of Spikenard, 66
Essential oils, distribution of,
  169
  how extracted, 171
  how formed, 170
Esters, 208
Evelyn on patches, 233
Evil odours of flowers, 157
Excessive use of perfumes, 87
Extract of Roses from Cyrene,
  67
  of Vine-leaves, 66
Eye-paint, Egyptian, 21

Fabulous stories of Sabians, 30
False rumour of plague in 1760,
  136
Ferene, 152
Fixatives, 205
Florence essences, 97
Florentine laboratory, 95
Florida Water, 147
Flowers cultivated in S. France,
  154
  in sick-rooms, 138
  odorous in sunshine, 156
  offered to the dead, 76
  that yield their perfume at
  night, 156
  used for garlands, 71
Fra Angiolo Paladini, 96
France, perfumes of, 99
Frangipani, 97
  flower, 98
  gloves, 98
  story of, 97
Frankincense offered to Bel, 24
Friar's Balsam, 178
Fumigating pastilles, 58
Fumigation for plague, 135
  to drive away demons, 51
Fumigations and incense, 9

R

INDEX

Gabrielle d'Estrées, 102
Galbanum, 9
Garden of Eden, 3
Genetic functions, 219
Geranium oil, 180
Gillyflower esteemed by the Arabs, 36
    perfume of the Greeks, 63
Ginger-grass perfume, 69
Glove-making in France, 109
Gold and frankincense offering, 9
    dust for the hair, 227
"Golden Rose," 98
    blessed by the Pope, 98
Great Plague of London, 134
Greek dry perfumes, 24
    love of flowers, 71
    perfumed bath, 72
    perfumers' colouring for perfumes, 64
    perfumes for clothes, 65
    perfumes for wine, 74
    perfumes made from the flowers, 65
    pot-pourri, 74
    unguents for the head, 69
Greeks and cosmetics, 227
    great liking for perfumes, 59
Griquas' method of adornment, 235
Grocers' Company, 89
Guests anointed with perfumes, 14

Habenaria bifolia, 156
Hair powder, 127
Hâtsepsu, Queen of Egypt, 22
    Expedition to Punt, 22
    gifts for, 22
Headache caused by perfume, 65
Healing essences, 75
Hebrew women and use of cosmetics, 226
Heliogabalus's love of perfumes, 83
    passion for roses, 83
Heliotrope, 181
Heliotropin, 209
Henry VIII's perfume, 163
Herba Bella donna, 230
Hesperis tristes, 156

Hindu marriage ceremony, 39
    sweet-smelling flowers, 40
    worship, perfumes offered, 39
History of Prince Arthur, 131
Holland, odorous bulbs, 155
"Holy anointing oil," 43
"Holy perfume," 43
Homer refers to perfumes, 59
Honey Water, 146
Horse-shoe vetch, 158
Houris, 32
Hungary Water, 140
    tradition of its origin, 140

Imperial Water, 146
Incense and prayer, 52
    early use by the Hebrews, 46
    how it was compounded, 50
    how it was offered, 48, 50
    origin of its use, 51
    recipe for making, 58
    sticks, 54
Incense used by ancient Mexicans, 55
    by Babylonians, 50
    by Buddhists, 54
    by Chinese, 55
    by Egyptians, 48
    by Jains, 54
    by Japanese, 55
    by Romans, 53
    in ancient Greece, 52
    in Christian Church, 56
    in Churches of Rome, 57
    in India, 53
India, perfumes used in, 38
Indian Nard, 46
Indians of Thompson River, 51
Iris, 184
    of Elis, 66
Italy famous for its perfumes, 96
Izaak Walton, 122

Jábir-Ibn-Hayyán, 30
James I orders floor to be rubbed with rosemary, 148
Japanese perfume, 42
Jasmine, 40, 181
Jewish Kings anointed, 43
Jews trade in spices, 43
Jinko, 42

242

"Jockey Club," 171
Judith, 44
Juniper, 8
  smoke to sweeten rooms, 127
Juvenal on cosmetics, 84

Karnak, inscription on walls, 12
Kei Islanders' fumigation to
  drive demons away, 51
Khaleefeh El-Mutawekkel, 33
  monopolises the rose, 33
King and Queen of Hanover,
  167
King Edward I's offering, 9
King of El-Heereh monopolises
  the anemone, 36
King George IV's perfume bills,
  167
  perfumes, 166
King Richard I, 159
King William IV, 167
Kohl, 225
Krishna, 177
Kyphi, 9, 16, 21
  Damocrates' recipe for, 17
  fame of, 16
  offered to Rā, 50
  recipes for making, 16, 17
Kypros, 63

La Cour parfumée, 106
Lamas of Tibet, incense used
  by, 55
Lasting odours, 63
Lavender cultivation in England, 141
  earliest allusions to, 141
  for linen, 122
Lavender Water, 142
  as medicine, 115
  early recipe, 115
  recipe, 142
Lavender-seller's cry, 143
Law introduced against patches,
  233
  proposed against the lure of
  perfumes, 151
Layard's description of Garden
  of Eden, 4

Lemery and civet, 204
Letters fumigated during the
  Plague, 135
"Life Elixir," 96
Lilac, 182
Linalol, 210
Lip-stick, composition of, 232
Liquid myrrh, 8
London spicers, 90
Lord John Russell, 168
Lord Palmerston, 168
Louis XIV and his love of per-
  fumes, 105
Lupin seeds for the skin, 85
Lure of patchouli, 222
  of perfume, 219
  of red hair, 220
Lychnis vespertina, 156

Madame de Pompadour's bills
  for perfumes, 106
Madame Tallien's bath, 108
Maiden plum, 157
Maimonides and origin of in-
  cense, 47
Malays of Johore, incense used
  by the, 52
Marie Antoinette's perfumes, 106
"Marie Antoinette" Perfume,
  160
"Marie Joséphine" Perfume,
  160
Marjoram from Kos, 66
Marquesas Islanders' cosmetics,
  237
Martial on "golden hair," 229
  on perfumed unguents, 86
"Mattiac balls," 229
Medes, love of perfume, 28
Medicinal properties of per-
  fumes, 66
Megaleion and its composition,
  64
Megallus, Greek perfumer, 67
Mendesium, 17, 67
  composition of, 17
Mercutio Frangipani, 97
Methyl anthranilate, 209
  benzoate, 210
Metopian, 17, 66
Mignonette, 182

INDEX

Milton's description of Garden of Eden, 3
Mohammed's favourite flower, 34
love of perfumes, 31
Monastic gardens, 95
"Moonlight of the Grove," 40
Mosque at Kara Amed, 32
of Zobaide, 32
Mouse mushroom, 157
Musk, 193
antiquity of, 195
artificial, 210
in medicine, 198
Musk pods, 195
caddy, 196
"catty," 196
how collected, 195
Musk-cat, 193
Musk-deer, 196
hunting the, 196
Muskone, 198
Muslims of India, incense used by, 54
Myrrh, 7, 8, 182
earliest record of, 8
how collected, 182
Myrtle, rival to the violet, 35
Mysteries of Osiris, 23

Nahuas, incense used by, 56
Napoleon's fondness for Eau de Cologne, 164
perfumer's bills, 164, 165
perfumes, 164
Nardinum, 82
Nardostachys, 46
Native fondness for odours, 238
Negroes, fondness for perfumes, 234
Neroli, 183
origin of name, 183
Nero's love of perfumes, 78
Nicolas de Montant, 104
Nicostratus, 72
Ninon de Lenclos, 106
Nioi-bukooroo, 42
Nitro-benzene, 206
Noorjeehan Begum, 39
discovers Attar of Rose, 40
Norton, Thomas, 92
Nubian perfumes, 235

Nyctanthes arbor tristes, 156

Odin the spicer, 90
Odour, conveyance of, 217
"Odour of sanctity," 130
Odours and colours, 156
as medicinal agents, 133
effect on animals, 221
of animal origin, 205
that nauseate, 216
that recall places, 215
Oil of Niobe, 210
of Redde Dog, 119
Old ledger of a Court perfumer, 167
Olfactory nerves, 212
Olibanum, 7, 179
how collected, 180
Omeltschenki's experiments, 139
Onycha, 9
Onyx perfume bottles, 68
Opoponax, 184
Orange-flower oil, 183
Orchidée, 209
"Ordinall of Alkimy," 92
Orris root, 184
Ovid alludes to floral offerings, 78
on beautifying the complexion, 85

Panathenaicum, 66
Paradise, description of, in Koran, 31
Paradise of Sumer, 7
Paris, sellers of perfumes, 99
Pastilles for perfuming the breath, 12
Patches, origin of, 232
Patchouli, 38, 185
as perfume for Indian shawls, 186
Patents granted to perfumers in France, 99
Peau d'Espagne, 160
Pepperers of London, 88
"Pepys letters," 96
Perfume against plague, 121
bellows, 127
for "any Prince," 121
for King Henry of France, 116
for the chamber, 120

Perfume found in Tutankh-
amen's tomb, 20
analysis of, 20
Perfume lamp, 120
necklace, 118
of a library, 147
of a toilet shop, 219
of Horus, 23
origin of word, 48
pan, 125
rings, 118
Perfumed bags, 115
candles, 57
cigarettes, 150
foods and sweetmeats, 13
Perfumed gloves, 99
for ye King, 109
introduced into England, 110
Perfumed pie, 32
skins, 109
Perfumer in London in seventeenth century, 91
Perfumers' advertisements, 152
immunity from cholera, 60
Perfumers of Paris, 99
Perfumes buried with the
mummy, 23
for snuff, 148
for the breath, 66
for the wrist, 69
for tobacco, 149
in cookery, 32
in the gymnasium, 26
in the Stuart period, 121
men like, 222
offered to Deities, 60
that affect emotions, 221
to purify the body, 36
used at Roman banquets, 83
used by the Greeks, 63
women like, 222
Peron, Greek perfumer, 67
Perry, 152
Persians, their love for roses, 27
Petit Grain, oil of, 184
Petunias, 156
Philadelphus coronarius, 158
Philippine Island perfumes, 236
Philonides, 71
Physical explanation of the
" odour of sanctity," 131
Piperonal, 209

Pitch and faggots burnt in the
streets, 135
Pleasurable odours, 216
Plumiera alba, 98
Poisoned by perfume, 104
Polynesian perfumes, 236
" Pomade Divine," 231
Poppœa's bath of asses' milk, 84
funeral, 78
" Poudre à la Maréchale," 105
Powder and patches, 232
Powder-puff and lip-stick, 231
Precious unguents, 18
Prince of Condé's snuff, 105
Princess Charlotte, 167
Princess Esterhazy and per-
fume, 166
Psagdi, 17, 72
Public fountains perfumed, 104
Punt, 10, 11

Qam'ey ointment, 17
Queen Alexandra, 168
Queen Elizabeth of Hungary, 140
Queen Elizabeth's fondness for
perfumes, 111
perfumed cloak, 111
perfumed gloves, 110
perfumes, 163
still-room, 111
Queen Olga of Greece, 168
Queen Victoria, 168
Queen of Würtemburg, 167
Quince perfume, 63

Rabbard's letter to Queen Elizabeth, 112
Recipe books, 116
for a perfume, first, 7
René the Florentine perfumer,
100
René's shop in Paris, 100
description of, 100
Réséda, 182
Rhazes, 30
Rhodium oil, 186
Richelieu's belief in perfumes,
106
Roman Catholics and use of incense, 57
dentifrice, 228
depilatory, 228

Roman Catholics—(*cont.*)
   face powders, 228
   hair dyes, 229
   lady's toilet, 228
   perfumers, 79
   perfumes, 81
   Thermæ, 79
" Roman odour " for snuff, 149
Romans and colour for cheeks
   and lips, 227
   and cosmetics, 84, 227
   favourite perfumes of, 87
Rondeletia, 159
Rondeletius, Gulielmus, 159
Rose, 171
   farms, 174
   of Persia, 172
   perfume of the Greeks, 63
Rosemary, 187
Roses of Kashmere, 39
   of Phaselis, 66
Rose-oil, distilled, 175
Rose-seller's cry, 173
Rose-sellers of Cairo, 34
Rose-water, first distilled, 31
   its soothing properties, 76
Rousseau on perfumes, 219
Rue, 187
   at the Old Bailey, 188
" Rushma " used in harems, 234
Russia leather, odour of, 147

Sabians and frankincense, 10
   fabulous stories of, 30
Sachet powder used by Queen
   Isabella of Spain, 117
Sacred tree, incense offered to,
   50
Sâdi's " Gulistãn," 27
Saffron perfume, 66
St. Anthony, patron saint, 89
St. Paul's Deanery fumigated,
   135
St. Teresa, 132
Sandal-wood, 7, 188
   antiquity of its use, 38
   used in embalming, 38
Santa Maria Novella, 95
Savage races, sense of smell, 214
Scented book, 147
   unguents for the body, 13
" Secrets of Alexis," 119

Seleucus II, 11
Sense of smell, 212
   fatigued, 216
Shadwell's description of strol-
   ling perfume-seller, 128
Shakespeare's allusions to
   flowers, 124
   favourite flowers, 123
Shells used as perfume con-
   tainers, 37
Smell of London, 215
Snuff perfumed, 148
Socrates on perfumes, 70
Solomon and Indian perfumes, 45
Solomon's pages, 227
Solon's law against use of per-
   fumes, 61
Spanish Skin, 160
Spicers' Guild, 88
Spicery in Oxford, 90
Spices for flavouring wines, 46
Spikenard, 189
   imported to Rome, 46
   its powerful odour, 45
   its value, 45
   recipe for ointment, 46
Spiræa ulmaria, 157
Stacte, 7
Stimulating odours, 222
Stinking hellebore, 157
Storax, 190
Story of Eau de Cologne, 144
Strewing floors with sweet
   rushes, 126
Strong odour of certain flowers,
   216
   odours, 218
Susinon, 63
   composition of, 82
Sweet-flag, 179
   perfume, 69
Sweet-pea, 186
Sweet-scented bath, 121
Synthetic perfumes, 208

Tahiti women and their per-
   fumes, 237
Taste and smell, 62, 213
Temple, Sir William, 223
Tessier, perfumer to the Em-
   peror, 165

Theophrastus on myrrh, 8
  on perfumes, 61
Thermæ of Caracalla, 79
  description of, 79
  frequenters of, 80
Tobacco as preventive of plague,
  136
" Tola pomatum," 235
Tonquin beans, 190
  musk, 196
Tracking enemies by smell, 214
Trained sense of smell, 94
Travelling perfume-seller, 128
Trees of Life, 7
Tritelia uniflora aspecus, 158
Tuberose, 190
Turquoise vases, 23

" Umari," a South-American
  Indian perfume, 237
Unguent of frankincense, 67
Unguents at banquets, 70
Urgujja, 41

Vanilla beans, 192
Vanillin, 207
Vapours, effect on brain, 218

Vases discovered in tomb of
  Tutankhamen, 19
  Roman, 82
Venice, trade in gums, 95
Verbena, 191
Vine-leaf perfume, 69
Violet, 191
  flowers, sherbet from, 35
Violets, odour of, 61
Vitivert, 192

Wars of the Roses, 173
" Water for odors most sweete,"
  112
West Indian civet, 204
White Violet perfume, 69
Willcocks, Sir W., on site of
  Garden of Eden, 5
" Wood Violet," 160

Xenophanes, 73

Yellow water-lily, 158
Ylang-ylang, 181

Zametti the Jew, 102